Tessa Lorant
The Secrets of Successful

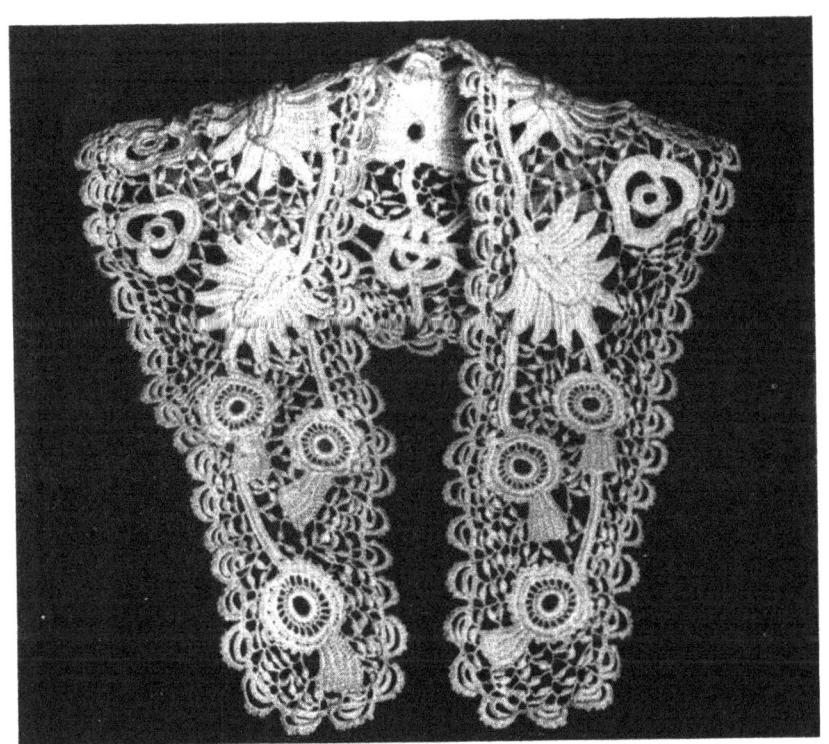

Rose, Thistle and Trefoil Collar.

Irish Crochet Lace

THE SECRETS OF SUCCESSFUL

IRISH CROCHET LACE

Copyright © Tessa Lorant 1985

The moral right of Tessa Lorant has been asserted

First published by The Thorn Press in 1985

Facsimile Edition published in 2014
ISBN 978-0-906374-53-5

THE THORN PRESS
WWW.THETHORNPRESS.COM

Contents

Page

Irish Crochet Terms	6
Irish Crochet Lace: Introduction	9
Shamrock Pincushion Cover	12
'Rosa Mundi' Doiley	14
Daisy Collarette	17
Emerald Isle Edging	20
Scrolled Dress Trimming	22
Vandyked Irish Rose Collar	24
Rose, Thistle and Trefoil Collar	32
Pineapple and Vine Dress Yoke & Vine Neckband and Cuffs Set	39
Baby Irish Crochet Lace Medallions	50
Christening Apron	59
Bolero	64

Techniques Section

Contents: Crochet Techniques	68
Crochet Techniques	69
Contents: Lacemaking Methods	80
Lacemaking Methods	81
Abbreviations	96

 CKNOWLEDGMENTS

I would like to express my sincere thanks to the three crocheters acknowledged below. Their cheerful enthusiasm in testing patterns and ideas has helped to make the research, writing and photography for this book a particularly worthwhile and satisfying project.

The following fine examples of Irish Crochet Lace were worked by Mrs Eileen Jones:
>The Rose, Thistle and Trefoil Collar
>The Vandyked Irish Rose Collar
>The Pineapple and Vine Dress Yoke
>The Vine Neckband and Cuffs Set
>The Daisy Collarette

This last is a very rudimentary form of Irish Crochet Lace, but it is nevertheless a delightful piece and an easy introduction to this form of lacecraft.

I would also like to thank Eileen for her help with arranging the sprig designs and for working through the patterns of the above pieces, as well as testing the instructions for the **Edgings.** I understand Eileen's enthusiasm for this beautiful craft goes back to childhood days, when she did a project on Irish Crochet in her sixth form year.

The following delightful garments were designed and worked by Mrs Helen Day:
>Christening Apron
>Bolero

Both pieces are based on traditional Baby Irish Crochet Lace medallions, but the two laces themselves are Helen's own interpretation of their use. Helen is an enthusiast for Irish Crochet; her charming designs do not lie idle in a drawer but are used for family occasions.

The following patterns were worked and checked by Miss Margaret Hitchcock:
>Shamrock Pincushion Cover
>Rosa Mundi Doiley
>Scrolled Dress Trimming
>Emerald Isle Edging

Margaret is a keen crocheter, and her beautifully executed work is a valuable and very welcome contribution to this book.

I would like to thank Mr Alexander, curator of the Guildford Museum, for permission to reproduce the Museum's photographs of some of their collection of Irish Crochet Laces.

The designs in this book are copyright and may not be used to make articles for sale.

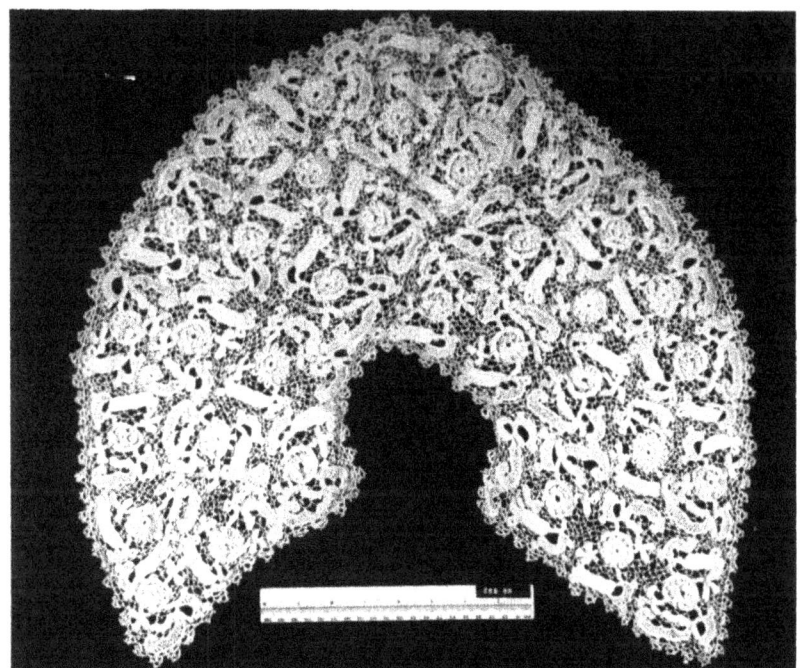
This large, ornate collar is dated 1850-1900. Photo: Guildford Museum.

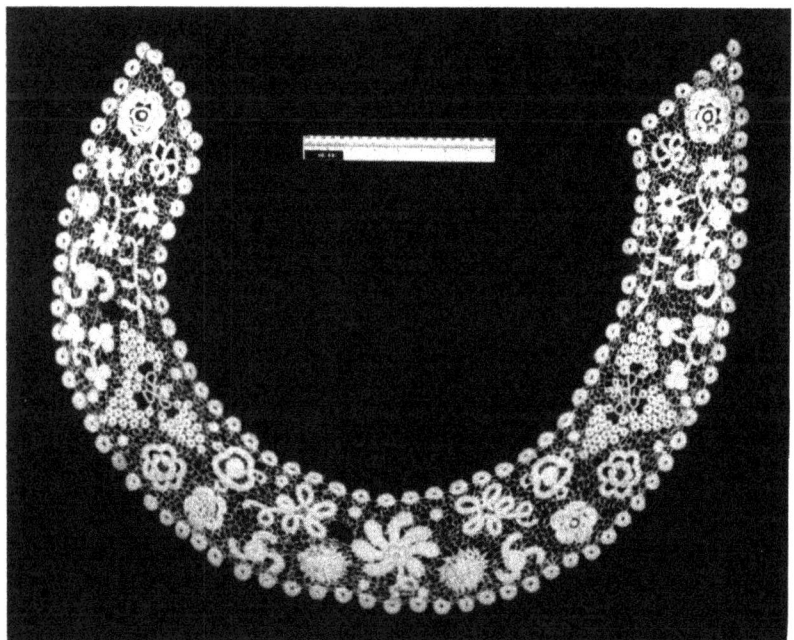
This late 19th Century collar, worked in silk cream thread, includes some unusual motifs.
Photo: Guildford Museum.

Irish Crochet Terms

Baby Irish Crochet was the term often used of a much lighter style of Irish Lace, using small motifs, often set into medallions, worked in fine, white yarn and trimmed with ribbons.

Banding is the term used for crocheting a chain space foundation row for the final lace edging. The banding is worked into the filling in such a way that it smoothly outlines the pattern shape.

Bars and Brides are the terms used of the fine crochet links connecting motifs.

Barrel is the name given to the straight part of the crochet needle which determines its size.

Bosses are heavily padded rings, thickly covered in double or treble stitches which may also be decorated with picots, to form motifs in their own right, or to be part of flowers or sprays.

Clones Crochet is Irish Crochet Lace from the area round the town of Clones, in County Monaghan. This form of Irish Crochet is distinguished by the use of some areas of filling between the sprigs, sprays or motifs, and also by the frequent use of the Clones Knot for filling or decoration.

The **Clones Knot** is a special, ornamental knot said to have been invented for Irish Crochet in the Clones region.

Cork Crochet differs from other forms of Irish Crochet Lace in that it has no network of crochet lace ground; the work is simply connected by brides or bars, occasionally worked in buttonhole stitch but most often in crochet. Designs have to be accurately drawn and accurately worked to fit the drawing.

Crochet Needle was the term used for what is now more commonly called a **crochet hook,** the tool used for crocheting. It provides a useful distinction in instructions where the hook part needs to be considered separately from the whole tool - the crochet needle.

Fillings are linked bar or bride patterns used to connect sprays or motifs secured on a pattern foundation.

Flax Thread was the term used for what is now called linen thread. Linen fibres come from the flax plant, at one time grown extensively in Ireland.

Guipure referred to lace in which the designs are held in place by brides or bars. This very general term was applied to all kinds of laces, bobbin as well as needlepoint, and eventually even applied to Irish Crochet Lace.

Lace Ground is the background of small lace spaces, usually called 'filling' in Irish Crochet Lace, which holds the motifs or sprays together.

Long Stitch is the old term for a double treble stitch.

Manlove's Thread was the thread, specially manufactured in Ireland, preferred above all others for making Irish Crochet Lace. Some references give it as made of cotton, others as made of linen fibres. Whatever the fibre content it was of high quality and available in very fine grades.

Mesh was the word used for the individual lace spaces in a lace ground. The word was also used to specify a gauge size for the bosses often made in Irish Crochet. Large knitting needles make good mesh gauges, but any cylindrical shape, including the left hand finger tips, can also be used.

Padding Cord is the term used of yarn to be crocheted over to help increase the relief structure which is such a feature of Irish Crochet Lace. The cord was traditionally made of smooth linen, dyed to the same shade as the crocheting yarn but of a heavier grade.

Pattern Foundation, sometimes aptly called **Emerald Foundation,** is the drawn or printed version of the design on a brown paper, stiff cambric or other fabric pattern shape. The completed motifs are secured to the foundation so that they are held in place firmly to allow the filling to be worked between the secured sprigs.

Plain is the old term for double crochet.

Powderings was the description applied to motifs, sprigs or sprays scattered rather haphazardly on the pattern foundation, leaving large areas empty for filling.

Shank is the name given to the narrowest part of the crochet needle, just before the hook.

Sprays or Sprigs are motifs connected together, often with stems, to form a naturalistic representation of various plants or emblems.

This blouse was started by a Mrs Bailey-Wells, of Little Brockhamhurst Farm, Betchworth, Surrey and finished by her daughter Kathleen in 1890. The yoke filling is Ardenza Point (a needlepoint filling) and the main body filling is buttonhole bars with picots. These could be replaced by Open Space Filling and Double Picot Bar Filling for a blouse worked entirely in crochet.

Victorian Blouse front. Photo: Guildford Museum.

Victorian Blouse back. Photo: Guildford Museum.

Irish Crochet Lace

'Irish' crochet has a very special place in two outstanding craft forms - the craft of short hook crochet, and the craft of lacemaking. I doubt if it is an exaggeration to say that Irish Crochet Lace, when made by a gifted worker, has the elements of an artform. A good example of Irish Crochet, worked in a crisp, fine yarn and with a fine, steel hook is not only exquisite to look at, it is unique because it has allowed free expression to the lacemaker's own artistry. The essence of the craft is that the lacemaker contributes her own ingenuity, and does not merely **follow** patterns but rather evolves her own adaptations as she works. It is not even necessary to count stitches, as in so much crochet, nor to follow a specific pattern, as in so much lacemaking. On the other hand, as with any other artform, there are examples of quite inferior Irish Crochet Lace, showing ungainly motifs cobbled together in a rather unpleasing way.

The freedom of expression which is so useful for Irish Crochet is, perhaps, one of the reasons that this type of crochet flowered so exuberantly in Ireland, a country noted for the wonderful imagination of its people. Ireland is well-known for many forms of lace apart from crochet lace: needlepoint, embroidery on net, Reticella work, pillow and appliqué laces, and exquisite rose point. And much of it is lovely, and of a very high standard. But it is Irish **crochet** lace that Ireland is famous for; it is **crochet** lace that Ireland brought to near-perfection, and it is Ireland's **crochet** lace that captivated and inspired so many English ladies to try their hand at this delightful craft, proudly showing their work at exhibitions held around the country. It is because of **their** enthusiasm that patterns were written down, and because of this that we can readily revive the tradition.

So what exactly **is** Irish Crochet Lace, and how did it come about?

Short hook crochet was, originally, simply one method of needlecrafting which could be used for making lace. It was also used in European convents to copy several of the more exotic laces such as Reticella and Point de Venise, and it could do this quite well, and was a faster method of lacemaking than the others.

During the earlier half of the nineteenth century a Mademoiselle Riégo de la Blanchardière discovered that Spanish Guipure Lace, a fairly heavy type of needlepoint with raised borders, could be copied in crochet both rapidly and most effectively. The basic needlepoint stitch is the buttonhole stitch, and this has a remarkably similar look to the double crochet stitch, particularly when the latter is worked in fine yarn and with a fine, steel hook. The raised edges were easy to imitate by the simple expedient of crocheting over a padding thread.

Mlle Blanchardière's first book of crochet lace patterns was published in the middle 1840s. The patterns came to the attention of Irish nuns, already known for their excellent lacemaking abilities. The Irish Crochet Lace industry is said to have begun in 1845, with the sisters of the Ursuline convent at Blackrock, County Cork. The nuns' interpretation of Mlle Blanchardière's patterns was so successful, and the girls at the convents learned it so well, that within a few years it spread from County Cork to the counties of Wexford, Sligo and finally to Monaghan, to the town of Clones in the North, which became as famous for its Irish Crochet as Cork City in the South.

But it was the distress caused by the great potato famine of 1847 which gave real impetus to the industry. Mlle Blanchardière's patterns were used by Irish ladies, themselves impoverished, to teach this type of lacemaking to the cottagers. These laces were then sold to fashion centres such as London, Paris and Vienna. For example, a Mrs W C Roberts, of Thornton, County Kildare, is said to have taught the poor how to make, and sell, their Irish Crochet laces, worked in the style of Guipure and Point de Venise. Though the industry did not survive in this area, several of the best lacemakers went to other lacemaking centres. One particularly gifted lacemaker went to Clones, to a Mrs Cassandra Hand, wife of the rector there. Between them they trained large numbers of local workers who, in due course, produced the crochet lace in many forms.

The ingenuity of some of the Irish workers produced a quite distinctive style of lace in its own right - **Irish Crochet Lace**. Several styles of Irish Crochet evolved in the different centres. Cork Crochet was renowned for the care with which it was planned, so that hardly any 'filling' or background lace was necessary, whereas Clones work, consisting of more of the rapidly made background lace, was less expensive, but featured the famous 'Clones Knot' which is said to have been invented there. The numbers of women involved in making this lace in the latter part of the century was 12,000 workers in the Cork region and 15,000 workers in the Clones region. The industry declined with changes in fashion and with the availability of mass-produced machine-made laces.

Though there are a few patterns to be found in the needlecraft journals of the late nineteenth century, Irish Crochet is not featured as much as knitting or ordinary short hook crochet. However, there was a great vogue for making Irish lace by amateurs, and some of the later journals, dating from the early 1900s, publish a number of traditional motif patterns.

The most popular thread used for making Irish Lace was Manlove's Irish Lace thread. This was available in as fine a size as 80, but was only recommended for amateurs in sizes 50, 42, 40 and even as coarse as 36, since it was considered too difficult for any but professionals to work the very fine threads. Trade workers used 1,000 yard reels, but Messrs Wm Briggs & Co Ltd put up special reels of 200 yards for amateurs, in white and écru. Smooth, linen padding threads were supplied by Messrs Harris & Sons, put up in skeins and dyed to match the colours of the Manlove's threads. Briggs also supplied silk Irish Crochet threads in black, white, cream and 'Paris', on 200 yard reels.

Though any ordinary fine, steel hook can be used for Irish Crochet, Briggs' specially made Cork Handled Crochet Hook was much preferred by the trade workers as it prevented cramp in the fingers, and remained cool however hard and long the crocheter worked. A further essential piece of equipment was the foundation on which Irish Crochet motifs were sewn before being joined by 'filling'. The firm of Briggs produced the aptly named 'Emerald Foundations', stiff green cambric printed with

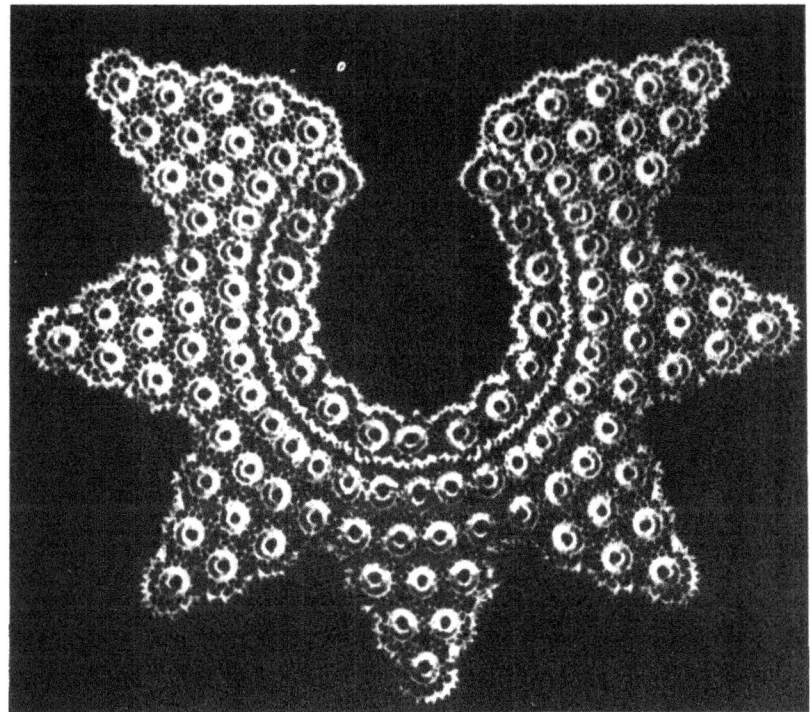
Daisy Collarette with seven points.

different patterns, for this aspect of the work.

None of these materials are now available; we have to make do with modern substitutes. In fact the quality of both threads and crochet hooks has increased considerably, so that the lack of traditional materials is not quite as bad as it might seem at first, though it is not possible to replicate Manlove's thread precisely. The 'woolly' cotton threads, which were said to spoil so much English work, were also said to spoil some of the 'foreign' as well as Irish work. All one can deduce is that the lace looks best when worked in a 'crisp' (that is a smooth, non-hairy) thread. And, like all lace, the finer the thread, the finer the resulting lace can be.

Fine, steel hooks are still readily available; the problem with these is that the handles are too fine for comfortable, long-lasting work. Plastic-handled crochet hooks **are** available, as mentioned under **Materials** on page 83.

In this book I have worked out, and elaborated on, techniques only briefly described in the old journals; I have tried to read between the closely packed pattern lines to revive what is undoubtedly a beautiful and not too difficult lacecraft, and to make it accessible to modern needlecrafters - even if they have never wielded a crochet hook before! I have also added what, I trust, will be found to be useful new ideas, inspired by the old patterns and illustrations. I hope you will add your own interpretations to what I have written down, and so increase the stock of the lacemaker's craft. Let our age, too, allow the flowering of craft at its best - making use of the new without in any way destroying the beauty of the old.

SHAMROCK PINCUSHION COVER

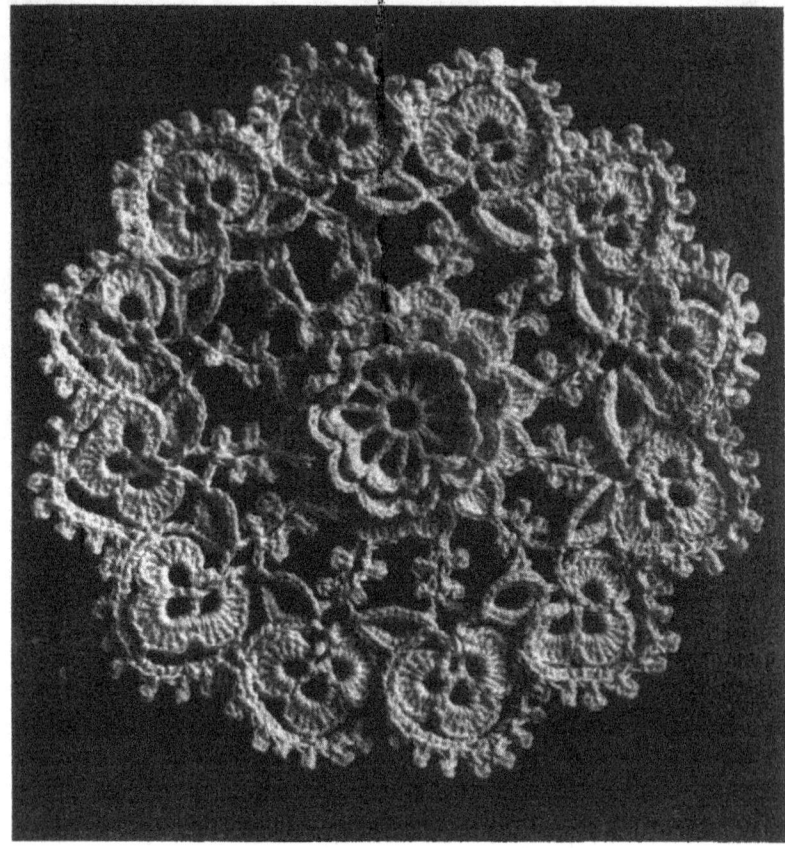

Materials:	Silver Gauge Category: 'Medium Fine Yarns'. Crochet hook sizes 1.00 mm - 2.00 mm.
Illustration:	Approximately 20g Southmaid Cotton, Cream. 1.25 mm steel crochet hook.
Measurements:	15 cm (6 ins) diameter, after washing.

This delightful little round was originally meant to be a pincushion cover. Pincushions are not much used now, but the piece could just as well be used as a doiley, or to decorate a dressing table. It is small enough, and made easily enough, to encourage the crocheter to go on to more ambitious projects, yet it is pretty enough to be worth making in its own right. Though the central flower has the texture of Irish Crochet, and though the outside motifs are shamrocks, there is no need for filling; this makes it a good project for a beginner.

PINCUSHION PATTERN:

The central rosette is worked first, then each shamrock complete with stalk and picots, is added to the tip of each flower petal.

The pattern is written out in detail to help beginners to this type of crochet. The rosette has layered petals, worked by double crocheting into the back of the stitch of the previous round. **Chain Picots** are made by working a length of chains, then double crocheting into the first of these chains: called **picoting into chain**.

Rosette:
Using the crocheting yarn, make 9 ch and ss to join into a ring.

Row 1: 7 ch (1st 4 ch count as 1st dtr), 1 dtr into ring, (3 ch, 1 dtr into ring)10, 3 ch, ss to join 4th of 1st 4 ch.

Row 2: (1 dc, 3 tr, 1 dc into each ch sp)12.

Row 3: 1 dc into the **back** of the dtr of Row 1, between the scallops made in Row 2, *4 ch, 1 dc*, working the dc into the **back** of the dtr of Row 1 each time.

Row 4: (1 dc, 5 tr, 1 dc into each 4 ch sp)12.

Row 5: 1 dc into **back** of 1st dc made in Row 3, *5 ch, 1 dc*, again working the dc into **back** of next dc of Row 3.

Shamrocks:
Row 6: Into 1st ch sp worked on Row 5 work: *1 dc, 4 tr, 6 ch, picot into 2nd ch, 6 ch, 1 ss into 2nd ch, 12 ch, 1 ss into 3rd ch; now work 18 dc **without** turning into the ch sp just made, join first and last dc with ss, 8 ch, 1 ss into 3rd ch, turn; make 5 ch, 1 tr into small ring, 4 ch, 1 tr in same ring, 5 ch, 1 dc into ring (so making 3 divisions), turn;

(1 dc, 9 tr, 1 dc)3, 1 dc in small ring, 6 ch, 1 ss into st next to picot, 5 ch, 1 ss into 1st ch, 6 ch, 1 ss into 2nd ch, 1 ch, 1 ss into 4th tr made at beginning of Row 6; 4 tr, 1 dc into same loop. Repeat from * all round the circle, but **join** ring of 18 dc to last pattern; work 9 dc, 1 ss into centre of adjoing bar of 6 ch, work 9 dc and finish as before.

Join last pattern to first. Fasten off.

Row 7: Begin at first petal of shamrock leaf and into centre work:
*1 dc, 9 ch, 1 dc into centre of second petal, 9 ch, 1 dc into centre of 3rd petal, 1 dtr in upper half of 18 dc worked on Row 6, repeat from * for each shamrock round circle.

Row 8: *(1 dc, 5 ch, picot into 1st ch)4 over 1st 9 ch sp, (1 dc, 5 ch, picot into 1st ch)3 over next 9 ch sp, 1 dc over same sp, 1 dc into next dtr. Repeat from * over the 9 ch sps round the circle and fasten off.

ROSA MUNDI DOILEY

Materials: Silver Gauge Category: 'Medium Fine Yarns'.
Crochet hook sizes 1.00 mm - 2.50 mm.

Illustration: Approximately 75g Southmaid 100% mercerized cotton in each of Cream, Shaded Pink and Shaded Springtime.
1.25 mm steel crochet hook.

Measurements: 27 cm (10.75 ins) diameter circular doiley.

This particularly simple pattern is an ideal introduction to the principles of Irish Crochet. Any beginner can learn to make it, and will be rewarded by an enchanting piece of crochet. The secret lies not only in the delightful crochet roses, but also in using a random-dyed cotton to achieve an old-fashioned 'Rosa Mundi' look.

The size of the doiley can be altered very easily. For a larger doiley, enlarge the central section by crocheting another round, say, and make more motifs to complete the larger circumference needed.

Another way of using this pattern is to use the roses, and possibly some leaves as well, as a decoration for a knitted or crocheted sweater, or even an outfit made of woven material. Work the roses in gold or silver for a really unusual decoration for a knitted or crocheted evening outfit, say.

Rose Motif

Leaf Motif

Rose Motif: (Make 8)
Using the Shaded Pink cotton, make six chain and join them into a ring.
Round 1: 3 ch, (2 ch, 1 tr into ring)5, 2 ch, ss into 3rd of 1st 3 ch made.
Round 2: *1 dc, 1 tr, 3 dtr, 1 tr, 1 dc* into every 2 ch sp. Join with ss.
Round 3: 3 ch, 1 dcb into every treble of **Round 1** (working at the back of the petals of Round 2).
Round 4: *1 dc, 2 tr, 5dtr, 2 tr, 1 dc into each 3 ch sp. Join with ss.
Round 5: 4 ch, 1 dcb into back of every double of **third** round.
Round 6: *1 dc, 2 tr, 7 dtr, 2 tr, 1 dc* into every 4 ch space. Join with ss.
Round 7: 5 ch, 1 dcb into back of every double of the **fifth** round.
Round 8: *1 dc, 2 tr, 9dtr, 2 tr, 1 dc* into each 5 ch space. Join with ss and fasten off.

Leaf Motif: (Make 8)
Using the Shaded Springtime Cotton, make 10 ch.
Row 1: Miss 2 ch, 7 DC, 3 DC all in last ch, 7 DC on **other side** of foundation chain.
Row 2: Turn; 1 ch, miss 1 st, 7 DC, 3 DC into next DC (forming base of leaf), 7 DC. Repeat Row 2 six more times.
Row 9: Turn; 1 ch, miss 1 st, 7 DC, 1 DC into base of leaf, 6 ch, miss 1 st, 5 DC on remaining ch, 1 DC into the stitch in which the DC before the 6 ch was worked, 7 DC down the side to finish the leaf. Fasten off.

Doiley Centre:

Using the Cream Cotton, make 10 ch; ss to join into a ring.
Round 1: 3 ch, 27 tr, ss last tr to top of 1st 3 ch.
Round 2: 5 ch, *miss 1st tr, 1 tr in next st, 2 ch*, ss into 3rd of first 5 ch.
Round 3: 6 ch, 1 tr into first 2 ch sp, *(1 tr, 3 ch, 1 tr) into next 2 ch sp*, ss into 3rd of 1st 6 ch.
Round 4: (3 ch, 1 tr, 2 ch, 2 tr) into 1st 3 ch sp, *2 tr, 2 ch, 2 tr* into next 3 ch sp. Join with ss to top of 1st 3 ch.
Round 5: (3 ch, 2 tr, 2 ch, 3 tr) into 1st 2 ch sp, *3 tr, 2 ch, 3 tr* into next 2 ch sp. Join with ss to top of 1st 3 ch.
Round 6: (3 ch, 2 tr, 2 ch, 3 tr) into 1st 2 ch sp, *1 ch, 3 tr, 2ch, 3 tr*. Join with ss to top of 1st 3 ch.
Round 7: Ss along top of 3 tr until next 2 ch sp, *(3 ch, 1 tr) into this sp, *3 ch, 2 dtr) in 1 ch sp, (3 ch, 2 tr) in 2 ch sp*. Join with ss to top of 1st 3 ch.
Round 8: Ss to sp after 2 tr, 5 ch, 1 dtr, 1 ch, 2 dtr into 3 ch sp. *3 ch, 2 dtr, 1 ch, 2 dtr* into each 3 ch sp. Ss into top of 1st 5 ch.
Round 9: Ss to first ch sp. *1 dc into next ch sp, 4 ch, 1 dc into next ch sp, 4 ch*. Ss to 1st dc. Fasten off.

DOILEY PATTERN:
Make the centrepiece, then the 8 **Rose** motifs and the 8 **Leaf** motifs.
There will be fifty-six 4 ch spaces. Join 2 rose petals and a leaf stalk as follows: *1 rose petal to a 4 ch sp, 2 free spaces, 1 rose petal to 4 ch sp, 1 free space, 1 leaf stalk to a free space, next space free*.

If you are reasonably skilled, you can join the motifs to the centrepiece as you are finishing them; work a rose and a leaf alternately. For the rose motifs, work to the last set of petals, then join 2 as shown in the illustration. For the leaves, work to the last row, then join to rose petals and centrepiece as shown in the illustration. You need to be clear that your motifs are the correct size for the centrepiece you have made.

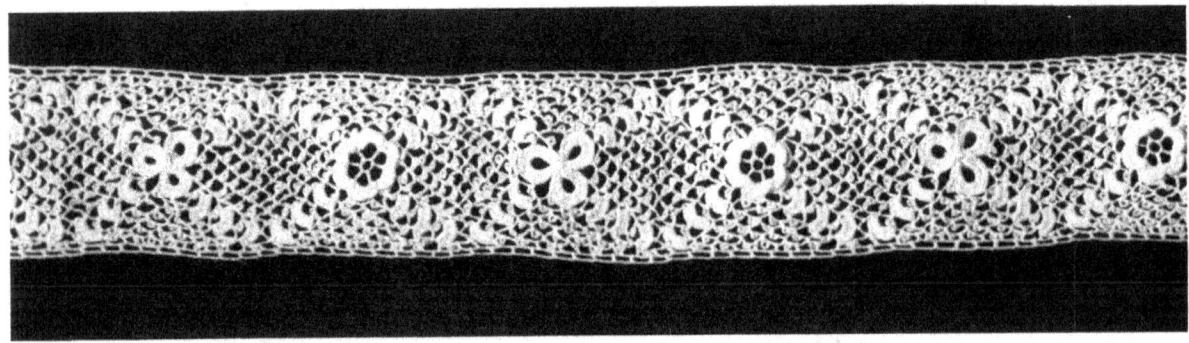

Early 20th Century Irish Lace. Photo: Guildford Museum.

Daisy Collarette

Materials:	Silver Gauge Categories: 'Fine' and 'Medium Fine Yarns'. Double Knitting cotton for padding, if liked. Crochet hook sizes 1.00 mm – 2.00 mm. Mesh gauges 7.00 mm – 8.00 mm knitting needles.
Illustrations:	125 g Silverknit 'Ideal' rayon. 1.00 mm steel crochet hook. 8.00 mm knitting needle as a mesh gauge.
Measurements:	**Neckline:** 56 cm (22 ins). **Depth:** 21 cm (8.25 ins).

This collarette provides an excellent introduction to making Irish Crochet Lace Collars. It is based simply on a large number of 'bosses' joined together with the simple **Open Space Filling** worked as the bosses are being finished. You cannot fail to become proficient in both these techniques by the time you have finished the collarette. The final banding and edging are both simple and good practice for more advanced work.

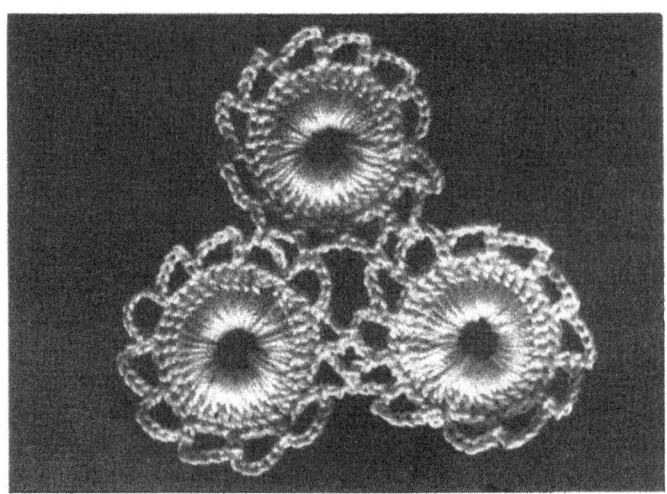
Three Bosses joined with Open Space Filling.

Daisy:
Using the crocheting yarn only:
Make a slip knot and first loop on the crochet needle; place the barrel of the crochet needle along the knitting needle and wind the yarn 20 or 30 times round this mesh gauge; wind it even more if you do not think the padding is thick enough.

Round 1: Yrh twice, and slip the padding off the top of the knitting needle, at the same time drawing one loop through the centre with the crochet hook. Make a fairly loose treble over the padding, and make 35 further trebles, joining the last to the first with a slip stitch.

Round 2: 1 dc in 1st tr, *6 ch, miss 2 sts, 1 dc* (12 ch sps); join to first dc and fasten off. This completes the first **Daisy**.

Using padding cord and crocheting yarn:
Make a slip knot and first loop with crocheting yarn on the crochet needle; place the barrel of the crochet hook along the mesh gauge, wind the padding cord 20 times round both, cut the padding cord and smooth it over the mesh, then continue as for working with crocheting yarn only.

Joining Daisies:
Row 1: Work a second **Daisy** like the first, but after **nine** chain spaces work: 2 ch, 1 dc over ch sp of the first **Daisy**, 3 ch, 1 dc on 3rd tr as before; 2 ch, 1 dc over adjoining chain space of the first **Daisy**, 3 ch, 1 dc on 3rd tr as before; 6 ch, join with ss to 1st dc. Fasten off.
Continue joining newly worked **Daisies** to those already worked until you have a row of 25 **Daisies**.

Row 2: Make a second row consisting of 24 **Daisies** exactly as Row 1, but join the **top two chain spaces** to the lower chain spaces of the **Daisies** of Row 1, as seen in the illustration. The 2nd row of **Daisies** will lie **between** those of the 1st.

Collarette Points: (6 points altogether)
The points of the collarette are simply worked as follows:

Row 3: Make 3 **Daisies** and place them between each of four sets of **Daisies** of Row 2, joining them as explained for that row.
Row 4: Make 2 **Daisies** and place them between each of the 3 **Daisies** of Row 3.
Row 5: Make 1 **Daisy** and place it between the 2 **Daisies** of Row 4.

Banding Row:
With right side of work facing you work into the 4 ch sps on top of each **Daisy** of Row 1:
1 dc, 4 ch, *(1 tr, 1 ch, 1 tr) in 2nd ch sp, (1 tr, 1 ch, 1 tr) in 3rd ch sp, miss 4th ch sp, miss 1st ch sp of next **Daisy** and repeat from *, finishing 4 ch, 1 dc in 4th ch sp of last **Daisy**.

Edging:
Row 1: *6 ch, 1 dc* in each ch sp round the outside of the collarette, up and down the points, finishing at the RHS edge. Fasten off.
Row 2: Rejoin yarn to LHS, 1 dc in 4 ch sp, *(1 dc, 3 tr, 3 ch, 3 tr, 1 dc) in each 6 ch sp*, finishing 1 dc in 4 ch sp on RHS.

Neckband:
Row 1: Work a row of 13 **Daisies**.
The neckband is now joined to the collarette by combining the 4 **lower** 6 ch sps (called 6 ch sp) on each of the **Daisies** on the neckband with the 1 ch sp between the two trebles (called 1 ch sp) in the neckline edging of the collarette as follows:
Row 2: With RHS facing you, 1 dc in 1st ch sp of neckband, *3 ch, (1 dc over 1 ch sp, 3 ch, 1 dc over 6 ch sp)4, repeat from * until the neckband is joined to the collarette neckline.
Row 3: Continue round neckband, working *6 ch, 1 dc* up the LHS of the neckband, across the top, down the RHS and join with ss to start.
Row 4: Working from R to L, *1 dc, 3 tr, 3 ch, 3 tr, 1 dc* in each 6 ch sp around the RHS, top and LHS of the neckband.
Row 5: Work *(1 dc, 1 tr) in 3 ch sp, (1 tr, 1 dc) in next 3 ch sp* over the neckband and collarette joining row. Ss to join and fasten off.

The collarette can be made larger or smaller by adding or subtracting multiples of 4 **Daisies** to the first **Daisy** row and working the following rows by adjusting the figures appropriately. Page 11 shows a collar worked in much finer yarn and with 7 points.

The illustrated collarette was worked in a shiny rayon yarn, in this case a deep burgundy colour. The yarn is not particularly fine, and if you find the 1.00 mm hook too difficult to work with, use a 1.25 mm or even a 1.50 mm one. The result will not be quite as dense, but you will nevertheless fashion a splendid collarette, adding a really striking accessory to your wardrobe. The burgundy colour looks outstanding over a light background; but you might consider making this collarette in a tinsel or glitter yarn to make yourself a crochet 'necklace'.

MERALD ISLE EDGING

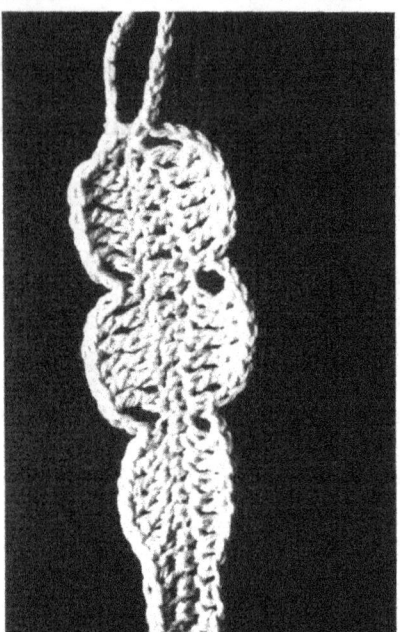

Leaf Motif   Thistle Motif

Materials: Silver Gauge Category: 'Fine Yarn'.
Crochet hook sizes 1.25 mm – 2.00 mm.

Illustration: One 20 g ball Coats Mercer Crochet 20, shaded green.
1.25 mm steel crochet hook.

Tension Depth: 5 cm (2 ins)
Length: One Leaf + One Thistle is 7.5 cm (3 ins).

This edging demonstrates how an Irish Crochet Lace outline can be formed by the motifs alone – the lower border needs no further edging. No filling is required, but the joins are a little harder than the ones in previous patterns.

Leaf Motif:
Make a 33 stitch foundation chain.
Core: Miss 1 ch, 13 dc, 8 tr, 2 dc. (Remaining chain will be used for top banding.)
First Side: 1 ch to cross the stem, and working down the other side of the foundation chain: 2 dc, (2 ch, 5 dtr, 2 ch, 1 dc)2, 1 ch, 5 tr, 5 ss; 1 ch to cross stem.
Second Side: Down other side of leaf work 5 ss, 5 tr, 1 ch, (1 dc, 2 ch, 5 dtr, 2 ch)2, 1 dc.

Thistle Motif:
Make a 28 stitch foundation chain.
Calyx: Miss 5 ch, 1 ss in 6th ch from needle to form a ring, turn, 1 ch to cross stem. (Remaining chains are left for stem and top banding.)
8 dc into ring, 1 ch to cross stem.
2 tr in next st, join to central tr in **Second Side** of **Leaf**, (2 tr in next st)4.
Head: 13 ch, turn this foundation chain to the right and join to last tr made, miss next st, 5 ss over 13 ch, (7 ch, join to same treble on **Calyx** as before, miss next st and work 5 ss on 7 ch)3, (3 ch, miss next st, 1 dc in between bars of thistle)4, 3 ch, 5 ss down side of thistle **Head**.
Finish **Calyx** by (2 tr in next st)4, 1 ss.
Stem: 2 dc, 2 ch, 2 dc, miss next 2 sts, 2 ss, 2 ch, 4 ss. (10 ch left).

EDGING PATTERN:
   Work the first **Leaf,** then continue with the first **Thistle** without fastening off.
Joining Leaf and Thistle:
   Continue the edging by working a further **Leaf**, joining the **First Side** of this **Leaf** to the **Thistle** worked just before it:
   (a) after the 1st double treble to the tr before last on the **Calyx;**
   (b) with the 10th double treble to the last 3 ch sp on the **Head.**
   Continue working the edging until it has sufficient length for your purposes; finish with a leaf for the best effect.

Banding Edge:
   Work 1 row of dc, working into each chain along the top of the motifs and connecting any separate motifs as you work.
   With right side facing, work *1 tr, 1 ch, miss next dc* to end of row.
This will give a slight curve to the edging.
For a straight edging, work 2 ch between the trebles on the banding row.

Emerald Isle Edging

SCROLLED DRESS TRIMMING

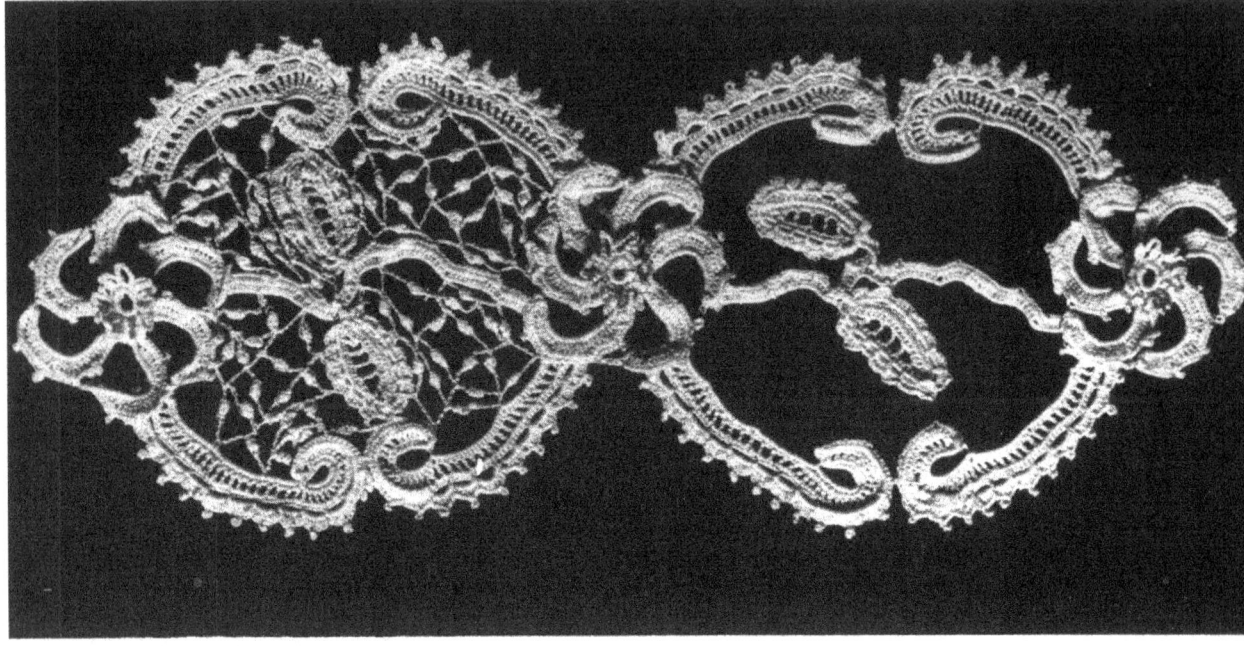

Two connected Scrolled Dress Trimmings. The left hand side trimming has a Clones Knot Filling; the right hand side trimming has been left blank and could be mounted over machined netting.

Materials:	Silver Gauge Category: 'Medium Fine Yarns' for crocheting. Silver Gauge Category: 'Medium Yarns' for padding. Crochet hook sizes .75 mm – 1.50 mm.
Illustration:	One 20 g ball Coats Mercer Crochet No 40. Double Knitting cotton for padding. 1.00 mm steel crochet hook.
Measurements:	23 cm (9 ins) wide (2 flower sprays); 14 cm (5.5 ins) deep.

This reasonably short trimming pattern shows how some Irish Crochet Lace needs no banding or edging of any kind; the sprays themselves, in this case the connected scrolls and flower heads, form the outline of the design. The amount of trimming needed for a particular project can be quite small, and a simple **Open Space Filling** could be substituted for the **Clones Knot Filling** illustrated. This design can also be mounted over a machined netting and the effect can be unexpectedly good.

Flower Spray: (P = 5 chain picot.)
Allow 36 cm (14 ins) 2-fold padding cord or 4-fold crocheting yarn for padding.
UCA, 24 dc and draw into a ring.

Petal:
Row 1: UCA, 1 dc, 25 tr, 2 dc, turn;
Row 2: (UC, 5 dc in next 5 tr, 1 P)4, UC, 6 dc into last 5 tr, LC, 1 dc, UC, 4 dc into centre ring. (Each petal takes up 4 dc on the ring.)

Work 5 more petals in this way, but join the **third** chain picot made into the 2 dc turn of the last petal. Fasten off.

Stalk and Leaves:
Row 1: UCA, 28 dc.
First Leaf:
Row 2: UC, 23 dc, turn; LC, 2 ch, miss 2 sts, 1 dc, (2 ch, miss 2 sts, 1 tr)5, 2 ch, miss 1 st, 1 dc (2 dc left for leaf stem), turn;
Row 3: 3 dc over each 2 ch sp, UCA, 2 dc, turn;
Row 4: UC, dc over last row of dc.
Cross leaf stem with 1 ss, passing the cord behind the stem.
Row 5: UC, 1 dc on next stitch of **Row 2**. *UCA, 4 tr, miss 4 sts of Row 2, UC, 1 dc into 5th st* to form edge all the way round the leaf.
Row 6: UC, 2 dc into leaf stem, UCA, 50 dc to form stalk, turn;
Row 7: UC, 44 dc over the last 44 sts (34 sts left unworked).

Make a **Second Leaf** like the first and UC, dc over the remaining 34 stitches of the stalk. TC to give the correct shape, fasten off and sew to flower behind a petal.

Flower Centre:
Wind yarn 30 times over a 5 mm (6s) knitting needle; dc into ring closely. Then form an edge by working *9 ch, miss 1 st, 1 dc* all round the ing. Sew this firmly to the centre of the flower.

Scroll:
Allow 30 cm (12 ins) 2-fold padding cord or 4-fold crocheting yarn for padding.
Row 1: UCA, 56 dc and join last 20 to form a ring, LC, turn;
Row 2: *1 ch, 1 tr* in stitches of last row, missing sts where necessary to prevent frilling on ring, turn;
Row 3: 2 dc over each ch sp, UC, turn;
Row 4: 20 dc into next 20 sts, (UCA, 3 tr, 1 P, UCA, 3 tr, miss 4 sts, UC, 1 dc)11. Fasten off.

TRIMMING PATTERN:
Give all the scrolls the same curve. Join the 2nd scroll to the first by joining it to the 10th stitch of the last row around the ring. Add any desired filling.

Vandyked Irish Rose Collar

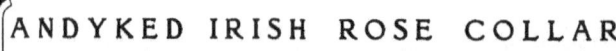

Materials: Silver Gauge Category: 'Very Fine Yarns'.
Crochet hook sizes .60 mm - 1.00 mm.

Illustration: Two 20g balls Coats Mercer Crochet Cotton No 40.
Size 0.60 mm steel crochet hook.

Measurements: **Neckband Edge:** 50 cm (19 ins).
Greatest Depth: 17 cm (6.5 ins).

Motifs: Greatest length by greatest width, excluding stems.
Fern Leaf: 8.5 cm x 5.5 cm (3.5 ins x 2.25 ins).
Rose Leaf: 6 cm x 5 cm (2.25 ins x 2 ins).
Rose: 3.5 cm (1.25 ins) diameter.
Star: 5 cm (2 ins) diameter.
Scroll: 4.5 cm x 4 cm (1.75 ins x 1.5 ins).
Small Flower: 2 cm (.75 ins) diameter.

One stage up from the previous collar, this design will really give you practice in making several types of unpadded motifs. The collar has an interesting outline, yet it isn't hard to make. The filling is the simplest possible, the edging is completely straightforward, but the result is a fine piece anyone would be proud to wear. Try it in silk if you feel confident enough.

Fern Leaf:
Please note that 1 ch is worked to cross the foundation chain for each leaflet; the instructions are given in detail for the first leaflet.

Complete Fern Leaf.

First Leaflet:
Make a 26 st foundation ch.
 Row 1: 1 DC in 2nd ch from hook, 1 DC in each of next 12 ch, 1 ch (to cross the stem), 13 DC up **other** side of chain, 1 dc into st at point.
 Row 2: 3 ch, 1 DC into 2nd ch from hook, 1 DC into next ch, 1 DC into **side** of dc worked into point, 1 DC into st at point, 13 DC, 1 ss into 1 ch worked to cross the stem, 1 ch, 17 DC, 3 dc all in next st (which is the centre point), 17 DC into each stitch down side of leaflet, 1 ss into 1 ch.

Second Leaflet:
Make a 22 st foundation ch.
Row 1: 1 DC into 2nd ch from hook, 1 DC into next 10 ch, 1 ch across stem, 10 DC up **other** side of chain, 1 dc into point.
Row 2: 3 ch, 1 DC into 2nd ch from hook, 1 DC into next ch, 1 DC in side of next st, 1 DC into point, 11 DC, 1 ss into 1 ch, 1 ch, 15 DC, 3 dc into point, 15 DC, 1 ss into 1 ch.

Third Leaflet:
Make a 20 st foundation ch.
Row 1: 1 DC into 2nd ch from hook, 1 DC into next 9 ch, 1 ch across stem, 9 DC up **other** side of ch, 1 dc into point.
Row 2: 3 ch, 1 DC into 2nd ch from hook, 1 DC into next ch, 1 DC into side of next st, 1 DC into point, 9 DC, 1 ss into 1 ch, 1 ch, 11 DC, 3 dc into point, 11 DC, 1 ss into 1 ch.

Fourth Leaflet:
Make an 18 st foundation ch.
Row 1: 1 DC into 2nd ch from hook, 1 DC into next 6 ch, 1 ch across stem, 1 DC up **other** side of ch, 1 dc into point.
Row 2: 3 ch, 1 DC into 2nd ch from hook, 1 DC into next ch, 1 DC into side of next st, 1 DC into point, 7 DC, 1 ss into 1 ch, 1 ch, 10 DC, 3 dc into point, 10 DC, 1 ss into 1 ch.

Fifth Leaflet:
Make a 22 st foundation ch.
Row 1: 1 DC into 2nd ch from hook, 1 DC into next 10 ch, 1 ch across stem, 11 DC up **other** side of ch, 1 dc into point.
Row 2: 3 ch, 1 DC into 2nd ch from hook, 1 DC into next ch, 1 DC into side of next st, 1 DC into point, 11 DC, 1 ss into 1 ch, 1 ch, 15 DC, 3 dc into point, 15 DC, 1 ss into 1 ch.
Stem: 1 DC into each of next 9 ch, working down stem to centre of **Fourth Leaflet**.

Sixth Leaflet:
Make a 10 st foundation ch.
Row 1: 1 DC into 2nd ch from hook, 1 DC into next 6 ch, 1 ch across stem, 7 DC up **other** side of ch, 1 dc into point.
Row 2: 3 ch, 1 DC into 2nd ch from hook, 1 DC into next st, 1 DC into side of next st, 1 dc into point, 7 DC, 1 ss into 1 ch, 1 ch, 10 DC, 3 dc into point, 10 DC, 1 ss into 1 ch, ss into base of **Third Leaflet**.
Stem: 10 DC down foundation ch to centre of **Second Leaflet**.

Seventh Leaflet:
Make a 12 st foundation ch.
- Row 1: 1 DC into 2nd ch from hook, 1 DC into next 8 ch, 1 ch across stem, 9 DC up **other** side of ch, 1 dc at point.
- Row 2: 3 ch, 1 DC into 2nd ch from hook, 1 DC into next st, 1 DC into side of next st, 1 dc into point, 9 DC, 1 ss into 1 ch, 1 ch, 11 DC, 3 dc into point, 11 DC, 1 ss into 1 ch, 1 ch, 1 ss into base of **Third Leaflet**.

Stem: 10 DC down foundation ch to centre of **Second Leaflet**.

Eighth Leaflet:
Make a 14 st foundation ch.
- Row 1: 1 DC into 2nd ch from hook, 1 DC into next 10 ch, 1 ch across stem, 12 DC up **other** side of foundation ch, 1 dc into point.
- Row 2: 3 ch, 1 DC into 2nd ch from hook, 1 DC into next ch, 1 DC into side of next st, 1 dc into point, 11 DC, 1 ss into 1 ch, 1 ch, 15 DC, 3 dc into point, 15 DC, 1 ss into 1 ch, 1 ch, 1 ss into base of **Second Leaflet**.

Stem: 10 DC down foundation chain to centre of **First Leaflet**.

Ninth Leaflet:
Make a 16 st foundation ch.
- Row 1: 1 DC into 2nd ch from hook, 1 DC into next 12 ch, 1 ch across stem, 1 ch, 13 DC up **other** side of ch, 1 dc into point.
- Row 2: 3 ch, 1 DC into 2nd ch from hook, 1 DC into next ch, 1 DC into side of next st, 1 dc into point, 13 DC, 1 ss into 1 ch, 1 ch, 17 DC, 3 dc into point, 17 DC, 1 ss into 1 ch, 1 ss into base of **First Leaflet**.

Stem: 12 DC down foundation chain; there are 2 extra sts on final length of stem than between each of the pairs of leaves. Fasten off.

Small Flower:
Make 6 ch and ss into first ch to form a ring.

Round 1: (1 dc, 4 ch)6 into ring; join with ss to first dc.

Round 2: Work (1 dc, 4 tr, 1 dc) into each 4 ch sp; join with ss to first dc. Fasten off.

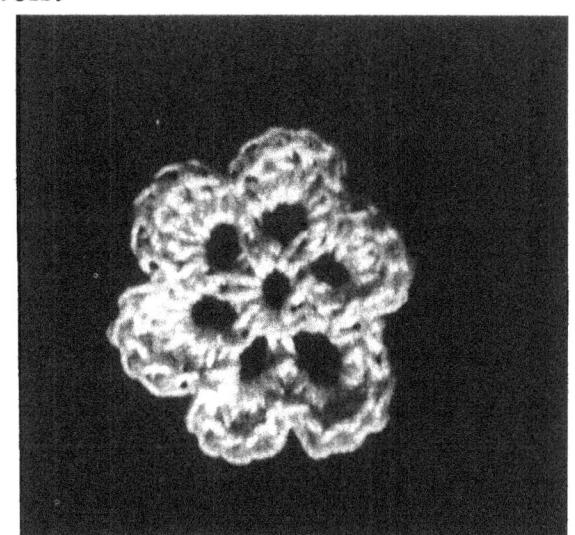

Small Flower.

Rose:
Make 6 ch; join with ss to form a ring.
Round 1: (1 dc, 4 ch)6 into ring; join with ss to 1st dc.
Round 2: (1 dc, 4 tr, 1 dc) into each 4 ch sp.
Round 3: (1 dcb into dc of Round 2, 6 ch)6.
Round 4: (1 dc, 6 tr, 1 dc) into each 6 ch sp.
Round 5: (1 dcb into dc of Round 4, 8 ch)6.
Round 6: (1 dc, 9 tr, 1 dc) into each 8 ch sp.
Round 7: (1 dcb into dc of Round 6, 10 ch)6.
Round 8: (1 dc, 11 tr, 1 dc) into each 10 ch sp.

Stem: Make 18 ch; 1 dc into 2nd ch from hook, 1 dc into each of next 17 ch; join with ss into **Rose** and fasten off.

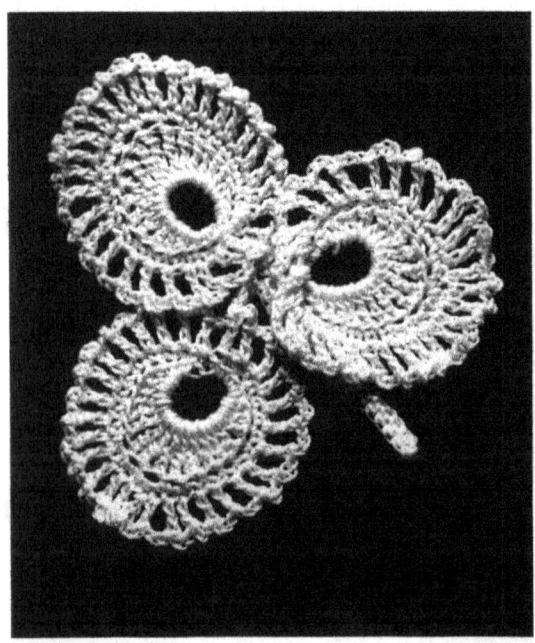

Rose Leaf with stem.

Rose with stem.

Rose Leaf:
First Leaflet:
Make a 13 st foundation ch and ss to join into ring.
Round 1: (3 dc, 3 tr, 3 dtr, 5 tr tr, 3 dtr, 3 tr, 3 dc) into ring and join with ss.
Round 2: 1 DC into each of the first 9 sts, 2 DC into each of next 2 sts, 3 DC into next st, 2 DC into each of next 2 sts, 1 DC into each of next 9 sts, join with ss into first DC.
Round 3: 6 ch, *1 tr into next st, 3 ch*, join with ss into 3rd of first 6 ch.

Second Leaflet:
Make a 22 st foundation ch; 1 dc into 13th ch from hook to form a ring.
Round 1: (3 dc, 3 tr, 3 dtr, 5 tr tr, 3 dtr, 3 tr, 3 dc) into ring just formed.
Round 2: 1 DC into each of the first 9 sts, 2 DC into each of next 2 sts, 3 DC into next st, 2 DC into each of next 2 sts, 1 DC into each of next 9 sts, join with ss into first DC.
Round 3: 6 ch, *1 tr into next st, 3 ch*, join with ss into 5th of first 22 ch.

Third Leaflet:
Make an 18 st foundation ch; 1 dc into 13th ch from hook to form a ring.
Round 1: (3 dc, 3 tr, 3 dtr, 5 tr tr, 3 dtr, 3 tr, 3 dc) into ring just formed.
Round 2: 1 DC into each of the first 9 sts, 2 DC into each of next 2 sts, 3 DC into next st, 2 DC into each of next 2 sts, 1 DC into each of next 9 sts, join with ss into first DC.
Round 3: 6 ch, *1 tr into next st, 3 ch*, join with ss into 1st of 18 ch.

Stem: 18 ch, 1 DC into 2nd ch from hook, 1 DC into each of next 17 ch and work 1 DC into each ch up to the central leaf. Fasten off.

Star:
Make 14 ch; ss in 1st ch to form ring.
Round 1: (1 dc, 7 ch)7 into ring; join with ss to first dc.
Round 2: Work 5 dc into each 7 ch sp; join with ss into first dc.
Round 3: (10 ch, 1 dc into 2nd ch from hook, 1 dc into next ch, 1 tr into each of next 3 ch, 1 dtr into each of next 2 ch, 1 tr in each of next 2 ch, miss 4 sts from Round 2, 1 dc in next st)7.
Round 4: Work around whole star point. {1 dc, 3 ch, miss 2 sts, (1 dc, 4 ch, miss 1 st, 1 dc)3, 4 ch, 1 dc into point, 4 ch, 1 dc into the same dc, (4 ch, miss 1 st, 1 dc)4}7; join with ss to 1st dc. Fasten off.

Star.

Scroll:

Make a 49 st foundation chain.

Row 1: 1 tr into 3rd ch from hook, 1 tr in same st, (2 tr into each of next ch)5, 1 dc into each of next 5 ch, 1 tr into each of next 2 ch, 1 dtr into each of next 3 ch, 1 tr into each of next 2 ch, 1 dc into each of next 10 ch, 1 tr into each of next 2 ch, 1 dtr into each of next 3 ch, 1 tr into each of next 2 ch, 1 dc into each of next 5 ch, (2 tr into each of next ch)6, 1 ch, ss into last ch.

Row 2: Work 1 ss up **other** side of each of first 15 ch, turn;
join with ss into the first ss, turn;
work 12 ss up **other** side of next 12 ch, turn;
(7 ch, 2 dc into next 2 ss)5, turn;
miss 2 dc, (1 dc, 7 tr, 1 dc into the 7 ch sp, miss next 2 dc)5, 20 ss into next 20 sts of foundation ch, turn;
join with 1 ss into 5th of the 20 ss just worked, turn;
19 ss.

Row 3:

Wheel:

11 ch, 1 ss into 8th ch from hook (forming a ring), turn;
3 dc into ring, 10 ch, 1 ss into 8th ch from hook, 1 dc into each of next 2 ch,
1 dc into ring, 11 ch, 1 ss into 8th ch from hook, 1 dc into each of next 3 ch,
1 dc into ring, 12 ch, 1 ss into 8th ch from hook, 1 dc into each of next 4 ch,
1 dc into ring, 11 ch, 1 ss into 8th ch from hook, 1 dc into each of next 3 ch,
1 dc into ring, 10 ch, 1 ss into 8th ch from hook, 1 dc into each of next 2 ch,
3 dc into ring, join with 1 ss into first dc into ring, 1 ss into each of next 6 sts, 2 dc into first 7 ch sp, 1 ss into 15th ss of 19 ss worked in Row 2, turn;
5 dc into same 7 ch sp as first 2 dc, 7 dc into each of next four 7 ch sps, 1 ss into next 6 sts, 3 ch, miss 24 st from Row 2, 5 ss into next 5 dc, turn;
1 ss into the 5th of the last 7 dc, turn;
1 ss into each of next 11 sts, 1 ch, 1 ss into last st. Fasten off.

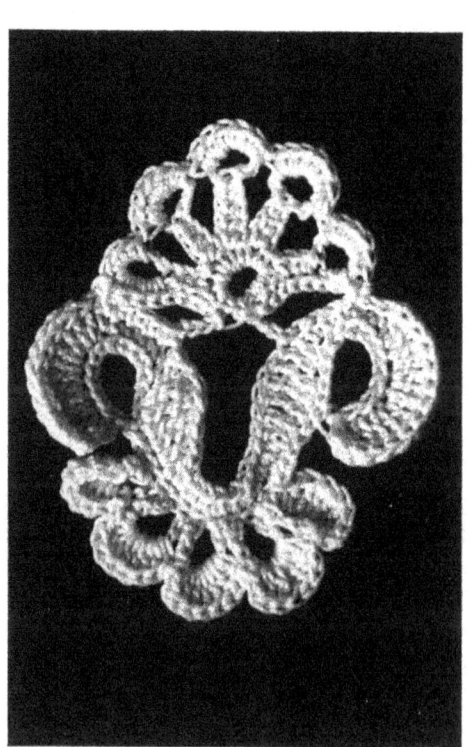

Scroll.

COLLAR PATTERN

Motifs Needed:
    6 Fern Leaves
    5 Rose Leaves
    5 Roses with Stems
    5 Roses without Stems
    3 Stars
    2 Scrolls
    27 Small Flowers

Collar Outline:
Work a foundation chain long enough to surround the complete collar outline as follows:
Make a multiple of 6 + 5 chain to surround the neck.
Work a picot chain: *(9 ch, 1 dc into 7th ch from hook to form a picot), 2 dc* to outline down one front, around the outside edge and up to the second front back to the neck. Ss to join. Attach this outline to the pattern foundation.

Filling:
Use the **Open Space Filling**, varying the length of chain to accommodate the different distances from the collar outline, as shown in the illustration.

Neckband Edging:
Row 1: Starting at the right hand side of the neckband, work a row of dc over the foundation chain surrounding the neckline.
Row 2: *5 dc, 3 ch, miss 1 dc*, 5 dc.
Row 3: 1 dc into each of first 5 dc, *(3 dc, 3 ch, 3 dc) into the 3 ch sp, miss 1 dc, 3 dc in next 3 sts, miss 1 dc*, (3 dc, 3 ch, 3 dc) into 3 ch sp, finish with 5 dc.

Outer Edging:
Ss to picot chain outline.
Row 1: Work *2 dc, (3 dc, 3 ch, 3 dc) into each picot*, 2 dc.
Ss to picot chain outline. Fasten off.

PATTERN DIRECTIONS:
Attach the motifs to the pattern foundation. Outline the collar shape as directed. Use the **Open Space Filling** composed of 5 ch bars to connect the motifs and the chain outline, but varying the lengths of the bars where necessary. Work the given **Edgings** around the collar outline.

Remove the collar from the pattern foundation.

ROSE, THISTLE AND TREFOIL COLLAR

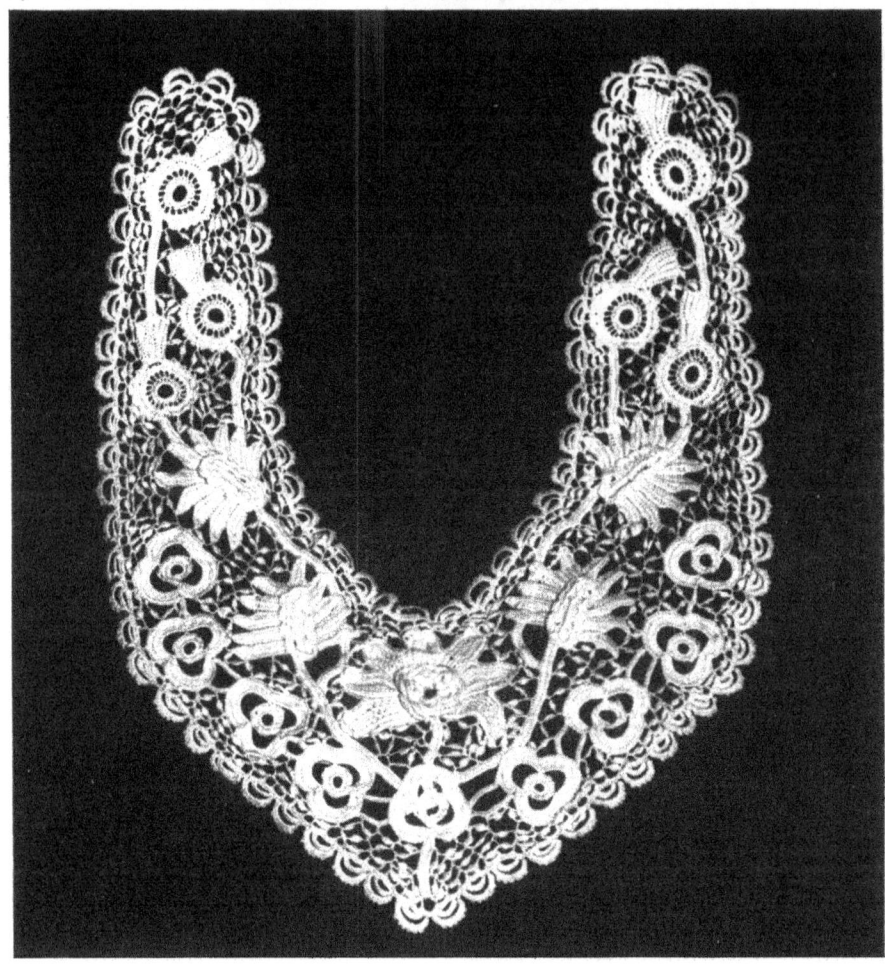

Materials:	Silver Gauge Category: 'Very Fine Yarns' for crocheting. Silver Gauge Category: 'Fine Yarns' for padding. Crochet hook sizes .60 mm - 1.00 mm.
Illustration:	Three 20g balls Coats Mercer Crochet No 40 crocheting yarn. One 20g ball Coats Mercer Crochet No 20 padding cord used 4-fold. .60 mm steel crochet hook.
Measurements:	**Outside Edge:** 89 cm (39 ins). **Inside Edge:** 55 cm (21.5 ins). **Depth:** 15 cm (6 ins) at widest point.

Motifs: Greatest length by greatest width, excluding stems.
Rose: 5 cm x 8 cm (2 ins x 3.25 ins)
Rose Centre: 3.5 cm (1.5 ins) diameter
Thistle: 5 cm x 3.5 cm (2 ins x 1.5 ins)
Trefoil: 3 cm x 3.75 cm (1.5 ins x 1.75 ins)
Rose Leaf: 5.5 cm x 6 cm (2.25 x 2.5 ins)

The entire collar is made up of just 5 motifs, none of which are in themselves particularly difficult to make. The filling given is the **Clones Knot** filling, and this is particularly attractive. However, any of the simpler fillings given in the **Techniques** section may be substituted.

The collar shape given here is, of course, just one interpretation of a collar pattern worked with these motifs. For example, you may wish to make a crochet collar for a dress - adapt the paper pattern to make the collar in Irish Crochet, using the motifs above.

This is an outstandingly beautiful lace collar. Make it finer by using Mercer Crochet No 60, or coarser using Mercer Crochet No 30, using a size of hook to suit. Naturally, your own tension may affect the size and shape, even if you use the materials quoted.

Padding Cord: Use the No 20 crochet cotton 4-fold as a padding yarn throughout.

Raised Rose Centre:
Allow approximately 40 cm (16 ins) 4-fold padding cord.
Round 1: UCA, 15 dc, TC. Join with ss into ring.
Round 2: (UCA, 10 tr, TC, 2 dc over cord and centre ring)5.
Round 3: (UCA, 16 tr, TC, 2 dc over cord and centre ring **behind** the join of last row of petals)5.
Round 4: (UCA, 20 tr, TC, 2 dc over cord and centre ring **behind** the join of last row of petals)5.
Round : (UCA, 24 tr, TC, 2 dc over cord and centre ring **behind** the join of last row of petals)5.
Fasten off and sew securely to centre of **Rose Motif**.
The centre will appear fuller if you moisten the shape and pull the petals up into a rose-centre shape.

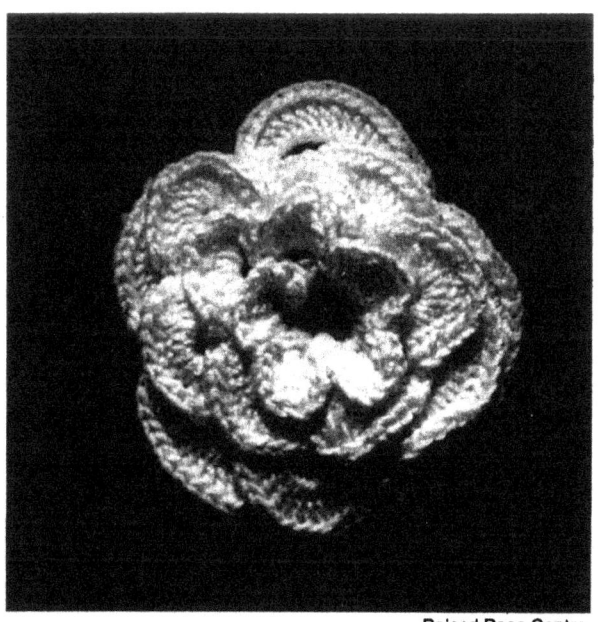

Raised Rose Centre.

Rose Motif:

The seven petals of this rose cluster round a central ring. The petals are spaced to lie flat and almost meet, the first and last joined by the stem between them. The raised centre is added later.

Allow approximately 75 cm (30 ins) 4-fold padding cord.

Ring: UCA, 37 dc, TC. Join into ring with ss.

First Petal Shape:
Row 1: UCA, 20 dc, LC.
Row 2: *1 ch, miss 1 dc, 1 dc*. Ss into centre ring; turn.
Row 3: *1 ch, 1 dc in 1 ch sp*; turn.
Row 4: *1 ch, 1 dc in 1 ch sp*. Ss into centre ring; turn.
Row 5: *1 ch, 1 dc in 1 ch sp*.
Row 6: Ss across top of petal to meet the cord. Ss into last st over cord; UCA, 2 dc.
Row 7: UC, *2 dc into each 1 ch sp*, UC 1 dc into centre of ring.

Second Petal Shape:
Row 1: UC, 3 DC, 9 TR into first 12 sts of First Petal Shape, UCA, 7 tr, 1 dc, LC; turn.
Row 2: 1 DC, 16 TR, 3 DC in last 20 sts, ss into centre ring, 1 ch; turn.
Row 3: 3 DC, 16 TR, 1 DC into next 20 sts, ss across top of petal to meet the cord. Ss into last st over cord, UCA, 2 dc to turn; turn.
Row 4: UC, *DC*.

Alternate First and Second Petal Shapes, joining each to the next in the first 12 sts, until 7 petals have been worked.

Petal Edging:
UC, dc to point of first petal, UCA, 1 dc, UC, dc to join of petals, 1 dc. Make last dc into the centre of the ring.
The edging can be worked **separately,** joined at the tips and joins of the petals. If you choose this method, be sure to make the edging long enough to lie flat round each petal.

Stem:
Row 1: UCA, 30 dc; turn.
Row 2: Miss 1st dc, TC, *1 DC*.
Fasten off.

Rose Motif with stem.

Trefoil:

Allow approximately 30 cm (12 ins) 4-fold padding cord.

Round 1: UCA, 20 dc, TC. Join into ring with ss.

Round 2: UC, 1 dc into each of next 4 sts, (6 ch, 1 dc into each of next 6 sts)2, 6 ch, 1 dc into next 4 sts.

Round 3: (UCA, 1 dc, 25 tr, 1 dc, UC, 1 dc into 3rd dc of next group of 6 dc)3. Ss to first dc of Round 2.

Round 4: UC, 1 DC into sts of previous round. At end of round work 1 dc over cord into Round 2 to make a firm join.

Stem:

Row 1: UCA, 30 dc; turn.
Row 2: 1 DC into next 12 sts, UCA 20 dc. Fasten off.

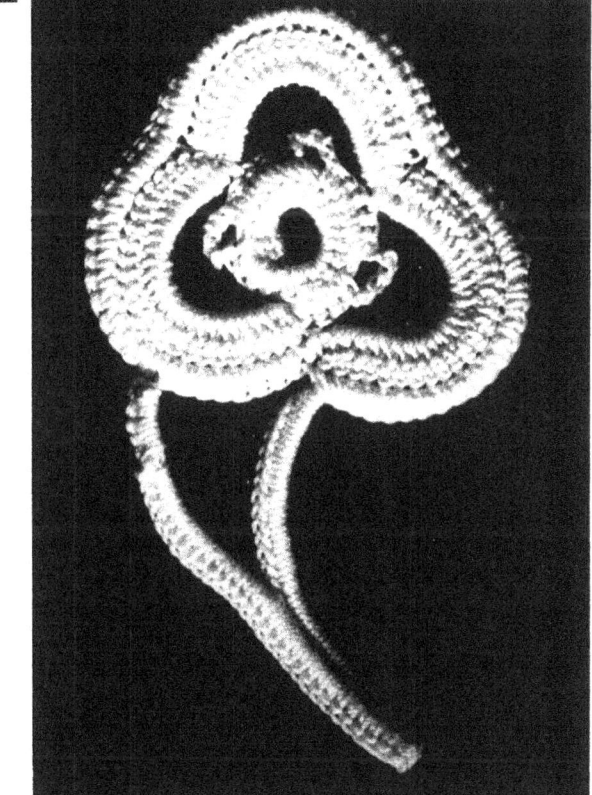

Reverse of Trefoil with stem, to show joins.

Thistle:

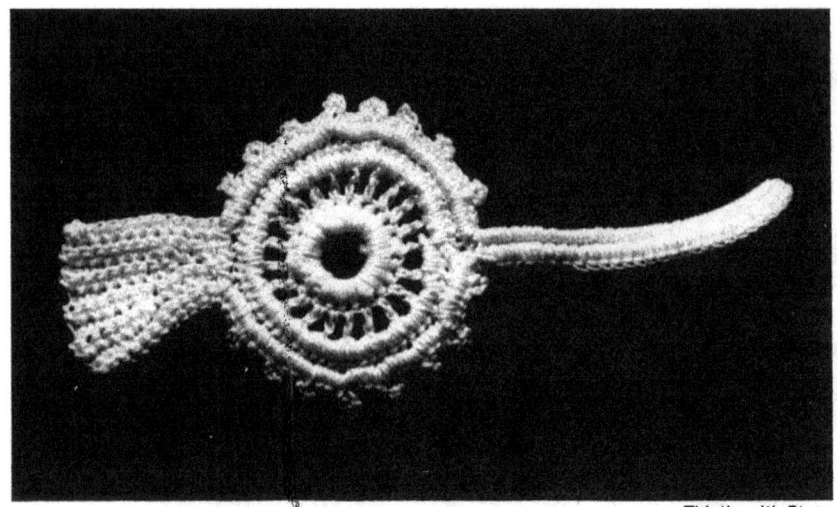

Thistle with Stem.

Allow approximately 20 cm (8 ins) of 4-fold padding cord.

Central Ring:
Wind crochet yarn 40 times round a 7.5 mm knitting needle together with crochet hook, place yarn round hook and pull through a loop. Make 20 dc into ring.

Thistle Centre:
Round 1: 4 ch, 1 tr into next st, *1 ch, 1 tr in next st*. Ss to third of first 4 ch.
Round 2: UC, *3 dc into 1 ch sp*. Ss into first dc.
Round 3: UC, (1 DC in next 3 sts, 4 ch, 1 DC in same st as last DC)8.
Work **Thistle Head** here:
Row 1: LC: 12 ch, 1 dc into 2nd ch from hook, 1 DC into each of remaining ch. 1 ss into next st of Round 2; turn.
Row 2: DC into next 11 sts, 1 ch; turn.
Row 3: 1 DC into next 6 sts, ss into next st; turn.
Row 4: 1 ss, DC to end, 1 ch; turn.
Row 5: 11 DC, 1 ss into Round 2; turn.
Row 6: 11 DC, 1 ch; turn. 8 DC, 1 ss into next st; turn.
Row 7: 1 ss, DC to end, 1 ch; turn.
Row 8: 11 DC, 1 ss into round 2; turn.
Row 9: 11 DC, 1 ch; turn.
Return to Round 3:
UC, (1 DC into each of next 3 sts, 4 ch, 1 DC into same st as last DC)8. Join with ss to first st of round.

Stem:
Row 1: UCA, work 30 dc over cord, 1 ch.
Row 2: LC: 1 DC in first st, TC. UC, *1 DC*. Fasten off.

Rose Leaf:

Allow approximately 100 cm (40 ins) 4-fold padding cord.

Short Stem: UCA, Work 65 dc.

Long Stem: UCA, Work 80 dc.

Leaf Centre:
Row 1: Continuing from stem and UCA, work 20 dc, 1 ch; turn.
Row 2: UC, 20 dc.

Leaflet One:
Row 1: UCA, 20 dc; turn.
Row 2: Miss first 2 sts, 1 DC, TC, 17 TR. Working on centre sts, miss 4 sts on leaf centre, 1 dc over centre cord into next st, 1 ch; turn.

Leaflet Two:
Row 1: UC, 12 DC over last leaflet, UCA, 8 dc; turn.
Row 2: Miss 2 sts, 1 DC, TC, 17 TR. Working on centre sts, miss 4 sts on leaf centre, 1 dc into next st, 1 ch; turn.

Work Leaflets Three and Four as Leaflet Two.

Leaflet Five:
Row 1: UC, 10 DC, UCA, 10 dc; turn.
Row 2: Miss 2 sts, 1 DC, TC, 17 TR. Working on centre sts, miss 4 sts, 1 dc into next st, 1 ch; turn.

Work leaflets Six and Seven this way, arranging them round the top of the leaf centre. Work Leaflets Eight, Nine and Ten as Leaflet Two.

Centre Ornament:
Row 1: UCA, 6 tr, 1 dc into first st of Leaflet One, (UCA, 6 tr, 1 dc into next dc joining leaflet to centre)10. UC, Work *DC* down side of stem. Fasten off. TC between each 6 tr set to raise the central scallops.

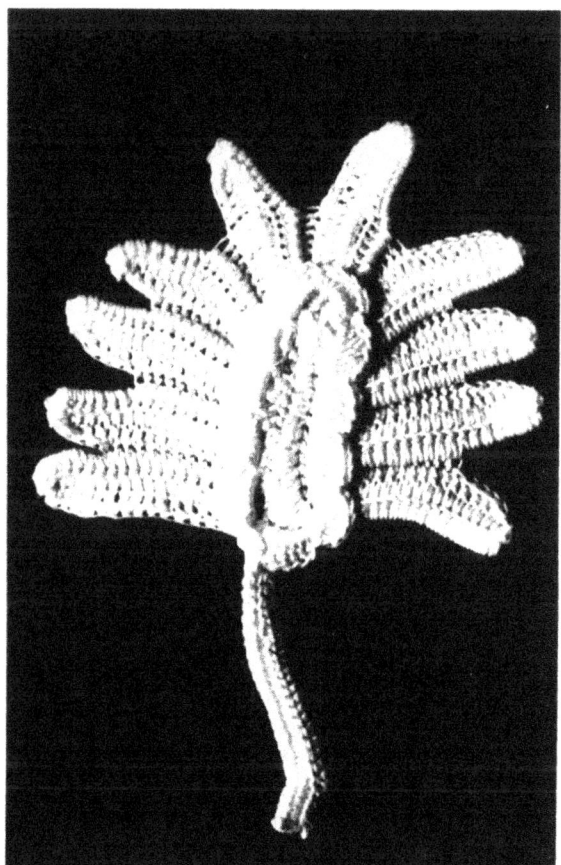

Rose Leaf with Centre Ornament and stem.

COLLAR PATTERN

Motifs Needed: 1 **Rose Motif** with 30 dc stem.
2 **Rose Leaves** with 65 dc stems.
2 **Rose Leaves** with 80 dc stems.
2 **Thistles** with 15 dc stems.
2 **Thistles** with 30 dc stems.
2 **Thistles** with 50 dc stems.
1 **Shamrock** with 30 dc stem.
2 **Shamrocks** with 20 dc single stems.
6 **Shamrocks** with split stems as given in pattern.

Filling: Clones Knot.

Edging: Feather Edging.

PATTERN DIRECTIONS:

Attach the motifs to the pattern foundation. Use **Clones Knot** or other filling to connect the motifs and to form the collar outline. Work the edging as follows:

Feather Edging: (Multiple of three 3 ch spaces worked on a {1 tr, 3 ch, miss 3 sts} band.)
Row 1: 6 ch, *miss 1 Clones Knot, 1 tr on other side of knot, 3 ch, 1 tr before next knot, 3 ch*. Join last 3 ch to 3rd of first 6 ch.
Row 2: **4 dc into each of the first two 3 ch sps, 2 dc into next sp; turn.
7 ch, 1 ss into 7th dc from hook; turn.
9 dc over 7 ch sp, 2 dc into same sp as last 2 dc; turn.
11 ch, 1 ss into first dc beyond 9 dc sp; turn.
6 dc into 11 ch sp, (3 ch, 3 dc into 11 ch sp)5, 3 ch, 6 dc into 11 ch sp.**
Repeat from: ** to ** all around collar. Fasten off.

You may find it simpler to form a chain outline before starting the filling. Attach the outline to the pattern foundation, add the filling and detach the collar from the foundation. Use the outline chain as a foundation row for:
Row 1: 6 ch, *1 tr, 3 ch, miss 3 ch space*, ss to 3rd of 1st 6 ch.
Now work Row 2 as above.

PINEAPPLE & VINE YOKE, CUFFS AND NECKBAND

Materials:	Silver Gauge Category: 'Very Fine Yarns' for crocheting. Silver Gauge Category: 'Fine Yarns' for padding. Crochet hook sizes .60 mm - 1.00 mm.
Illustrations:	Four 20 g balls Coats Mercer Crochet No 40 for yoke; two 20 g balls Coats Mercer Crochet No 40 for neckband and cuffs; two 20 g balls Coats Mercer Crochet No 20 for padding. .60 mm steel crochet hook.
Measurements:	
Yoke:	Front neck to centre front V: 29 cm (9 ins). Back Opening: 15 cm (6 ins).
Cuffs:	26 cm (10.25 ins) long by 10 cm (4 ins) wide.
Neckband:	40 cm (15.75 ins) long by 6 cm (2.5 ins) at the widest point.

M o t i f s:	Greatest length by greatest width, excluding stems.
Pineapple:	14 cm (5.5 ins) x 5.5 cm (2.25 ins).
Rosette:	7.5 cm (3 ins) diameter.
Vine Leaf:	7 cm (2.75 ins) x 8 cm (3.25 ins).
Bunch of Grapes:	Large: 5.25 cm (2.25 ins) x 4.5 cm (1.75 ins).
	Small: 4.25 cm (1.75 ins) x 4 cm (1.5 ins)
Trefoil:	Large: 5 cm (2 ins) along all three sides.
	Small: 4.5 cm (1.75 ins) along all three sides.

This exquisite dress yoke, with its matching cuffs and neckband, is designed round the natural sweep of the vine to set off the motifs. The yoke itself uses a fine pineapple spray as its centrepiece, with an ornately scrolled rosette below. This rosette is repeated on the cuffs, while the neckband is designed using smaller grape berries and with a small trefoil centre. A breathtakingly beautiful set which can be used for a long-sleeved dress or blouse.

White or écru crochet lace shows to best advantage over a dark background. Wear it 'transparent' to show off a bronzed skin, sewing it to the rest of the garment by hand, or tack it over dark velvet or silk taffeta for an outstanding effect.

A beginner could start with the neckband; this makes a handsome addition to any garment with a plain round neck or a stand-up collar. The experience of crocheting the neckband will give sufficient confidence to attempt the more ambitious cuffs, followed by the yoke.

Use the No 10 padding cord 4-fold throughout unless otherwise directed.

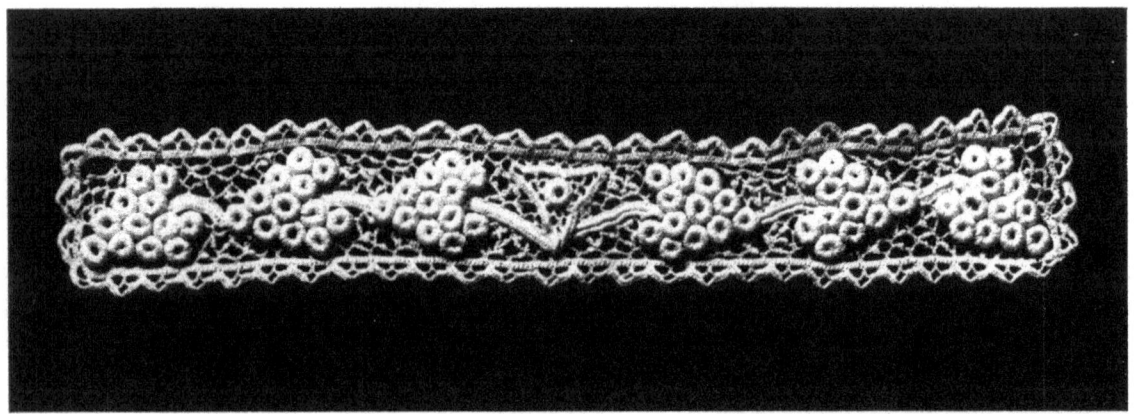

Small Bunch of Grapes and Trefoil Neckband.

Rosette:

The multi-petalled rosette is mounted on a solid base and surrounded by a coiled border to provide the lower central front spray. The coils will be evenly held in place by the single picot lace filling attached to each coil; **even out** the coils by passing an 8 mm (0) knitting needle through them.

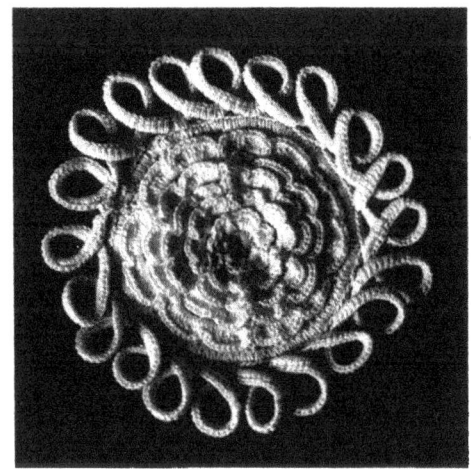

Rosette with Coiled Border.

Centre:
Using the padding cord 2-fold, make a single large loop with long ends.

Using the crocheting yarn:
Round 1: (1 dc, 3 tr, 1 dc)6 into ring. Pull on **both** ends of the padding cord to close the loop; this makes a firm, neat centre; ss to join.
Round 2: (5 ch, 1 dc into the **back** of the work between the scallops)6.
Round 3: {(1 dc, 5 tr, 2 dc, 5 tr, 1 dc) into 5 ch sp}6.
Round 4: (7 ch, miss 2 scallops, 1 dc into the **back** of the work between scallops)6.
Round 5: {(1 dc, 7 tr, 2 dc, 7 tr, 1 dc) into 7 ch sp}6.
Round 6: (9 ch, miss 2 scallops, 1 dc into the **back** of the work between scallops)6.
Round 7: {(1 dc, 9 tr, 2 dc, 9 tr, 1 dc) into 9 ch sp}6.
Round 8: (11 ch, miss 2 scallops, 1 dc into the **back** of the work between scallops)6.
Round 9: {(1 dc, 11 tr, 2 dc, 11 tr, 1 dc) into 11 ch sp}6. Fasten off.

Centre Underlay:
Using crocheting yarn, work 8 ch; join into ring with ss.
Round 1: 3 ch, 14 tr into ring. Join with ss to 3rd of first 3 ch.
Round 2: 3 ch, 2 tr into each tr. Join with ss to 3rd of first 3 ch.
Round 3: 3 ch, *1 tr in next tr, 2 tr into next tr*. Join with ss to 3rd of first 3 ch.
Round 4: 3 ch, *2 tr in next 2 tr, 2 tr in next tr*. Join with ss into 3rd of first 3 ch.
Round 5: 3 ch, *1 tr into each of next 3 tr, 2 tr in next tr*. Join with ss into 3rd of first 3 ch.
Round 6: UC, *1 dc into each of next 3 tr, 2 dc into next st*. Join with ss to first st. (75 sts altogether.)

Coiled Border Round:
Round 7: *UCA, 30 dc, twist work clockwise to fold back on itself, miss 4 dc; UC, 1 dc into next dc on Round 6*. Fasten off.

Sew the centre of the rosette firmly to the underlay, or see **Techniques** section.

Trefoil:

Large Trefoil:
Allow approximately 35 cm (14 ins) 4-fold padding cord, including centre.

Round 1: Wind the 4-fold padding cord 5 times round a 7.5 mm (1s) mesh together with the barrel of the crochet hook. LC. Remove the mesh, yrh and draw through the centre of the padding and make 1 ch over the cord, then make 1 ch; work over the padding cord to fill the ring with 29 dc. Join with ss to 2nd ch.

Round 2: *(7 ch, miss 2 dc, 1 dc in next st)3; turn. Ss to centre of first chain loop, 1 dc into ch sp, (7 ch, 1 dc into next ch sp)2; turn. Ss to centre of first ch sp, 1 dc into first lp, 7 ch, 1 dc into next ch sp. Fasten off by enlarging the loop on the hook and pulling the crochet yarn support through. Take the yarn to the next st in ring **allowing it to lie slack** against the side of the piece just worked - this loose yarn will be crocheted over later. Repeat twice more from *. Rejoin yarn to the base of the first 7 ch sp worked.

Round 3: {UC, (6 dc into each ch sp side)3; UCA, 15 dc; UC, **and** working over the loose yarn, (6 dc into each ch sp side)3; UC, 1 dc between leaflets}3. Join with ss and fasten off.

Small Trefoil:
Allow approximately 27 cm (11 ins) 4-fold padding cord, including centre.

Round 1: Wind the 4-fold padding cord 5 times round a 7 mm (2s) mesh together with the barrel of the crochet hook. LC. Remove the mesh, yrh and draw through the centre of the padding and work 1 ch over the padding, work 1 ch; working over the padding cord fill the ring with 26 dc. Join with ss to 2nd ch.

Round 2: *(5 ch, miss 2 dc, 1 dc into next st)3; turn. Ss to centre of first ch sp, 1 dc into first ch sp, (5 ch, 1 dc into next ch sp)2; turn. Ss to centre of first ch sp, 1 dc into first ch sp, 5 ch, 1 dc into next ch sp. Fasten off by enlarging the loop on the hook and pulling the yarn support through. Take the yarn to next st in the ring **allowing it to lie slack** along the side - the loose yarn will be crocheted over later. Repeat twice more from *. Rejoin yarn to the base of the first 5 ch sp worked.

Round 3: {UC, (4 dc into each ch sp side)3; UCA, 8 dc; UC **and** working over the loose yarn, (4 dc into each ch sp side)3; UC, 1 dc between leaflets}3. Join with ss and fasten off.

Bunch of Grapes:
The 12 grapes in the bunch are each made separately, then sewn together by starting with 1 grape in the 1st row, adding 2 grapes in the 2nd row, 3 in the 3rd row and 4 in the 4th row. Add the remaining 2 grapes between the first 2 and the last 2 of the preceding row, leaving a space in the centre. The stem is sewn into this space.

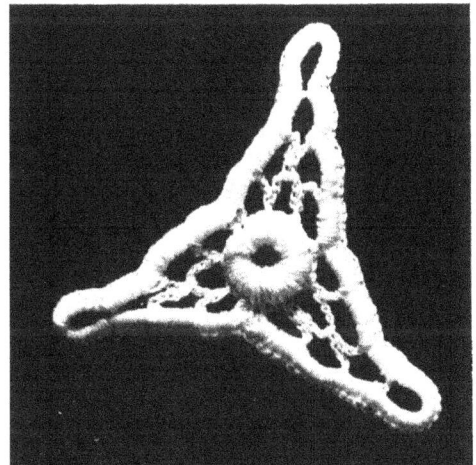
Trefoil.

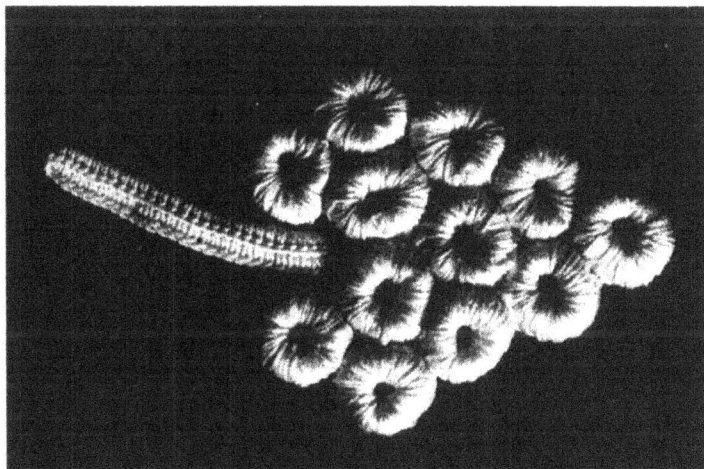
Bunch of Grapes with Stem.

Allow approximately 20 cm (8 ins) 2-fold padding cord for each stem.
The **size** of the grapes, and consequently of the bunch of grapes, is determined by the size of the mesh gauge used to make the centre. The grapes for the designs illustrated here were made using 7.5 mm (1s) and 7 mm (2s) knitting needles as mesh gauges.

Grape: (Make 12)
Wind the (single) padding cord 20 times round the straight part of a knitting needle of the appropriate size together with the barrel of the crochet hook. Remove the knitting needle, hook the crocheting yarn through the central space and make 1 ch over the padding, plus another ch; now work over the padding and fill the ring with double crochet. Work another round of double crochet **over** the first padded round, again filling the ring completely. Ss to join. Fasten off.

Stem:
Use the padding cord **2-fold**; now fold the length in half to make a 4-fold cord, working the first dc over the fold. This anchors the cord securely.
Row 1: UCA: 1 dc into fold, 32 dc; TC; LC, 3 ch; turn.
Row 2: Miss 1st dc, UC, *1 DC*. Fasten off.

The stem can be **curved** by pulling on the padding cord as required; pull each thread separately to avoid puckering.

Experienced crocheters can double crochet the grape being worked to previously worked grapes while working the second round of dc.

Vine Leaf:
Large Leaflet:
All approximately 40 cm (16 ins) of 4-fold padding cord.
Make 22 ch with crocheting yarn.

Row 1: UC, 1 dc into 2nd ch from hook, *1 dc*; UCA, 5 dc; UC, *1 DC* into **other** side of each foundation chain; UCA, 5 dc; UC, 19 DC; UCA, 5 dc; turn.
Row 2: Miss 1st 5 dc; UC, 19 DC; TC; UCA, 5 dc; UC, 22 DC; UCA, 5 dc; turn.
Row 3: Miss 1st 5 dc; UC, 23 DC; TC; UCA, 5 dc; UC, 20 DC; UCA, 5 dc; turn.
Row 4: Miss 1st 5 dc; UC, 23 DC; TC; UCA, 5 dc; UC, 24 DC; UCA, 5 dc; turn.
Row 5: Miss 1st 5 dc; UC, 27 DC; TC; UCA, 5 dc; UC, 22 DC; UCA, 5 dc; turn.
Row 6: Miss 1st 5 dc; UC, 26 DC; TC; UCA, 5 dc; UC, 25 DC, UCA, 5 dc; turn.
Row 7: Miss 1st 5 dc; UC, 27 DC; TC; UCA, 5 dc; UC, 2 DC, LC, 2 ss. Fasten off.

Medium Leaflet:
Allow approximately 30 cm (12 ins) of 4-fold padding cord.
Make 17 ch with the crocheting yarn.

Row 1: UC, 1 dc into 2nd ch from hook, *1 dc*; UCA, 5 dc; UC, *1 DC* into **other** side of each foundation chain; UCA, 5 dc; UC, 13 DC; UCA, 5 dc; turn.
Row 2: Miss 1st 5 dc; UC, 16 DC; TC; UCA, 5 dc; UC, 16 DC; UCA, 5 dc; turn.
Row 3: Miss 1st 5 dc; UC, 18 DC; TC; UCA, 5 dc; UC, 19 DC; UCA, 5 dc; turn.
Row 4: Miss 1st 5 dc; UC, 18 DC; TC; UCA, 5 dc; UC, 16 DC; UCA, 5 dc; turn.
Row 5: Miss 1st 5 dc; UC, 21 DC; TC; UCA, 5 dc; UC, 2 DC; LC; 2ss. Fasten off.

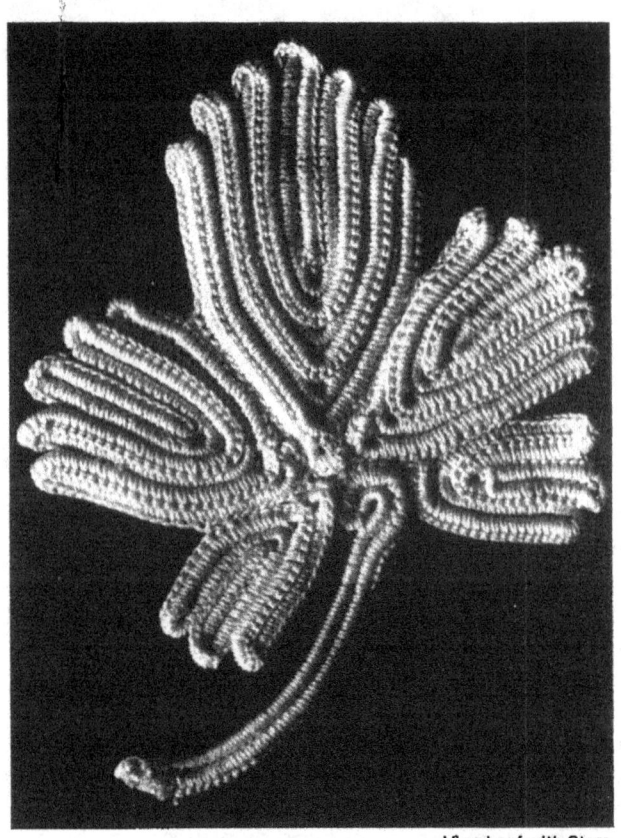

Vine Leaf with Stem.

Small Leaflet:
Allow approximately 20 cm (8 ins) 4-fold padding cord.
Make 13 ch with the crocheting yarn.
Row 1: UC, 1 dc into 2nd ch from hook, *1 dc*; UCA, 5 dc; UC, *1 DC* into other side of each foundation chain; UCA, 5 dc; UC, 11 DC; UCA, 5 dc; turn.
Row 2: Miss 1st 5 dc; UC, 13 DC; TC; UCA, 5 dc; UC, 12 DC; UCA, 5 dc; turn.
Row 3: Miss 1st 5 dc; UC, 15 DC; TC; UCA, 5 dc; UC, 2 DC; LC; 2 ss. Fasten off.

Stem:
Allow approximately 10 cm (4 ins) 4-fold padding cord.
Row 1: UCA, 50 dc; turn.
Row 2: Miss 10 dc, 1 dc into base of next dc; UCA, 4 dc; turn.
Row 3: Miss 4 dc; UC, 2 DC into each of next 8 dc, 1 DC into each dc to end of stem.
Fasten off.

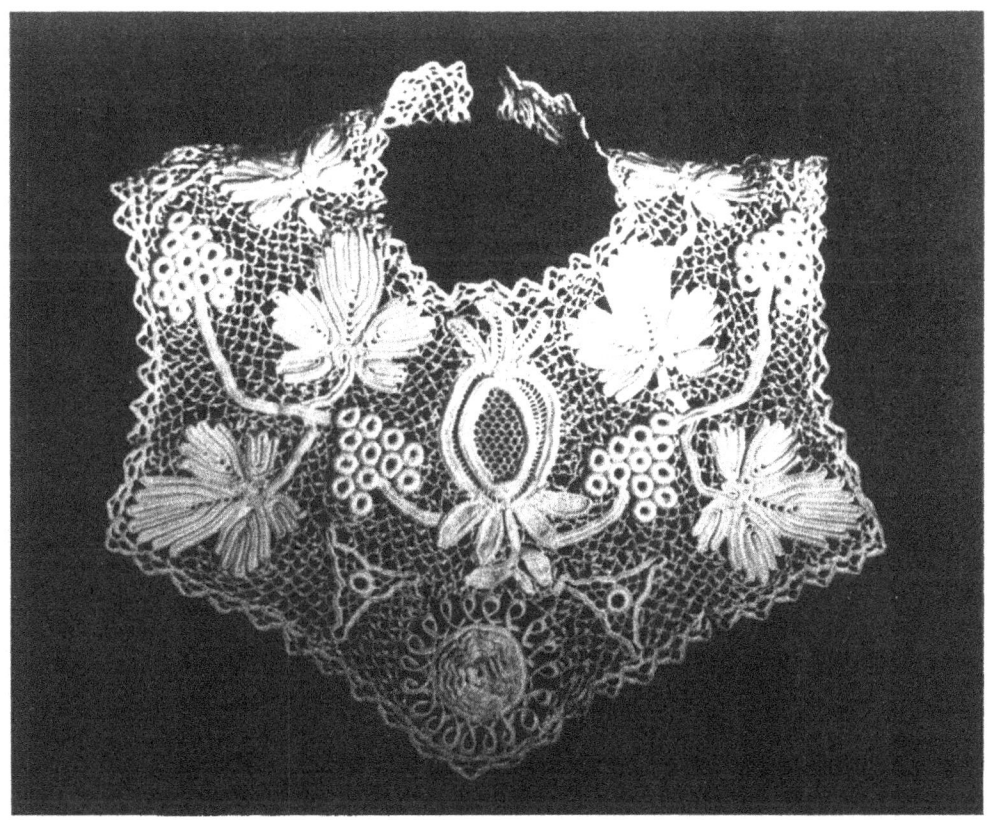

Front of Pineapple Yoke.

Pineapple Spray:

This large, ornate spray is the centrepiece of the yoke and is placed at the upper centre front to show to greatest advantage. The spray is built up from several pieces, with a highly textured oval to highlight the central lace.

Use the padding yarn 4-fold, except where instructed otherwise.

Lace Centre:

Using the crocheting yarn, make 6 ch and join with ss into a ring.

Row 1: 5 ch, 1 dc into ring, 3 ch, 1 dc into ring; turn.
Row 2: 5 ch, 1 dc into 3 ch sp, 3 ch, 1 dc into 5 ch sp; turn.
Row 3: 5 ch, 1 dc into ch sp, 3 ch, 1 dc into next ch sp, 3 ch, 1 dc into **same** ch sp as last dc; turn.
Row 4: 5 ch, 1 dc into ch sp, (3 ch, 1 dc into next ch sp)2, 3 ch, 1 dc into **same** ch sp as last dc; turn.
Row 5: 5 ch, 1 dc into next ch sp, (3 ch, 1 dc into next ch sp)3, 3 ch, 1 dc into **same** ch lp as last dc; turn.
Row 6: 5 ch, 1 dc into next ch sp, *3 ch, 1 dc into next ch sp*; turn.
Row 7: 5 ch, 1 dc into next ch sp, *3 ch, 1 dc into next ch sp*; turn.
Row 8: 5 ch, 1 dc into next ch sp, (3 ch, 1 dc into next ch sp)4, 3 ch, 1 dc into same ch lp as last dc; turn.
Row 9: 5 ch, 1 dc into next ch sp, (3 ch, 1 dc into next ch sp)5, 3 ch, 1 dc into **same** ch lp as last dc; turn.
Row 10: 5 ch, 1 dc into next ch sp, *3 ch, 1 dc into next ch sp*; turn.
Row 11: 5 ch, 1 dc into next ch sp, *3 ch, 1 dc into next ch sp*; turn.
Row 12: *1 dc into first ch sp, 3 ch, 1 dc into next ch sp*; turn.
Row 13: *1 dc into first ch sp, 3 ch, 1 dc into next ch sp*; turn.
Row 14: *3 ch, 1 dc into next ch sp*; turn.
Row 15: *3 ch, 1 dc into next ch sp*; turn.
Row 16: *1 dc into first ch sp, 3 ch, 1 dc into next ch sp*; turn.
Row 17: *1 dc into first ch sp, 3 ch, 1 dc into next ch sp*; turn.
Row 18: *1 dc into first ch sp, 3 ch, 1 dc into next ch sp*; turn. Fasten off.

Stalk with Two Leaves: (turn at the end of each row)
Row 1: UCA, 16 dc (to be used later); UCA, 15 dc.
Row 2: LC, (3 dc, 7 tr, 4 dc, 1 ss) into last 15 dc made.
Row 3: 3 dc, 5 tr, 3 dc, 1 ss; UCA, 4 dc to turn, 3 ss, 3 dc, 5 tr, 3 dc, 1 ss; UCA, 4 dc.
Row 4: UC, 15 dc along edge of leaf, 1 ss into last st on stalk; UCA, 20 dc.
Continue by working with **Lace Centre** as follows: PINEAPPLE:
Round 1: Take up the **Lace Centre** and, beginning at the base and UC, work 4 dc into each ch sp side all round the shape. Ss to first dc to join.
Round 2: LC, 7 dc, (1 ch, miss 1 st, 1 tr in next st)26, 14 dc, (1 ch, miss 1 st, 1 tr into next st)26, 7 dc; ss to first dc to join; turn.
Round 3: 1 dc, (1 ch, miss 1 st, 1 tr in next st)33, 8 ss, (1 ch, miss 1 st, 1 tr in next st)33.
Round 4: UC, (2 dc into each 1 ch sp)31;
  First Leaf:
  UCA, 20 dc; LC; turn.
  3 ch, miss 2 dc, *1 tr, 1 ch, miss 1 dc* to end of leaf; ss to Round 3; turn.
  2 dc into each 1 ch sp, 4 dc into 3 ch sp; UCA, 4 dc; turn.
  Miss 4 dc, dc down other side of leaf, ss into next st on Round 3.
  Second Leaf:
  UCA, 24 dc; LC; turn.
  3 ch, miss 2 dc, *1 tr, 1 ch, miss 1 dc* to end of leaf; ss into Round 3; turn.
  2 dc into each 1 ch sp, 4 dc into 3 ch sp; UCA, 4 dc; turn.
  Miss 4 dc, dc down other side of leaf, ss into next st on Round 3.
  Third Leaf:
  UCA, 20 dc; LC; turn.
  3 ch, miss 2 ch, *1 tr, 1 ch, miss 1 dc* to end of leaf; ss into Round 3; turn.
  2 dc into each 1 ch sp, 4 dc into 3 ch sp; UCA, 4 dc; turn.
  Miss 4 dc, dc down other side of leaf, ss into next st on Round 3.
Round 4: UC, (2 dc into each 1 ch sp)31.
Stalk with Two Leaves Continued:
Row 5: UC, 10 dc along other side of stalk; UCA, 15 dc; LC; turn.
Row 6: 3 dc, 7 tr, 4 dc, 1 ss; turn.
Row 7: 3 ss, 3 dc, 5 tr, 3 dc, 1 ss; UCA, 4 dc; turn.
Row 8: Miss 4 dc, 1 dc into each st on other side of leaf, 1 ss into stalk; UC, 1 dc into each dc to end of stalk; fasten off.
Four Lower Leaves:
Row 1: UCA, 20 dc; turn.
Row 2: LC, 3 dc, 16 tr, 1 dc; turn.
Row 3: 3 dc, 15 tr, 2 dc; UCA, 4 dc; turn.
Row 4: TC; UC, *1 dc*.
Repeat Rows 1 - 4 to make a second leaf.
Row 9: UCA, 4 dc.
Repeat Rows 1 - 4 twice more to make two more leaves. Fasten off.
Sew the 4 leaves in place, 2 on either side of the stalk, placing the 4 dc **behind** it.

Round 5: Using the padding cord **12-fold**, dc from the second lower leaf on the RHS to the base of the first upper leaf; turn.
LC, *7 ch, miss 3 dc, 1 dc into next dc* to end of padded dc just worked. Fasten off.
Rejoin yarn to LHS of the three upper leaves. UC (12-fold), dc down to the LHS lower leaf; LC; turn.
7 ch, miss 3 dc, 1 dc into next dc to end of padded dc just worked. Fasten off.

Central Ornament

Make a loop of padding cord to fit the first row of padded dc surrounding the **Lace Centre.** Cut a cardboard piece to fit half the length and, using this as a template, wind the padding cord 24 times round it. Take the padding off the template and cover it with closely spaced double crochets. Fasten off, leaving enough yarn for sewing. Bend the padded ring into the correct shape, then stitch it to the pineapple centre, taking care that no sewing stitches show on the right side of the work.

Outline Cord

Allow the appropriate length of padding cord for the outline, as given in the patterns below. Using crocheting yarn, work the first dc over the fold to anchor the cord, then cover the 2-fold cord with dc. TC to correct length. Join with ss to first dc and fasten off.

Vine Leaf and Rosette Cuff.

CUFFS PATTERN

Motifs Needed:
: 4 **Vine Leaves** with 20 dc stems.
  2 **Rosettes**
  2 x 66 cm (26 ins) 2-fold padding cord covered in dc.

NECKBAND PATTERN

Motifs Needed:
: 1 Small **Trefoil**.
  2 Small **Bunches of Grapes** with 33 dc stems.
  2 small **Bunches of Grapes** with 20 dc stems.
  2 small **Bunches of Grapes** with 20 dc stems.
  85 (33.5 ins) 2-fold padding thread covered in dc.

YOKE PATTERN

Motifs Needed:
: 1 **Pineapple Spray**.
  1 **Rosette**.
  6 Large **Trefoils**.
  6 **Vine Leaves** with 50 dc stems.
  2 **Vine Leaves** with 40 dc stems.
  2 **Bunches of Grapes** with 79 dc stems.
  2 **Bunches of Grapes** with 69 dc stems.
  2 **Bunches of Grapes** with 39 dc stems.
  2 **Bunches of Grapes** with 34 dc stems.
  200 cm (79 ins) 2-fold padding covered in dc.

Filling:
: **Single Picot Lace**.

Edging: (Multiple of 11 dc stitches)
*(5 ch, miss 4 dc, 1 dc into next dc)2, 1 ch; turn.
ss to centre of 5 ch sp, 2 dc into this 5 ch sp, 5 ch, 1 dc into next 5 ch sp, ss into last 2 ch to base of sp, 1 ch; turn.
5 dc into first 5 ch sp, 7 dc into next 5 ch sp, 5 dc into last 5 ch sp, 1 dc into next dc. Repeat from * all round each piece.

PATTERN DIRECTIONS:

Attach the motifs to the basic pattern shapes. Outline each shape with a band of 2-fold padding covered with dc. Use **Single Picot Lace** or other filling to connect the motifs and the yoke, neckband and cuff outlines. Work the given **Edging,** or any other you may prefer, around each pattern piece.

If you prefer to outline the shapes with a simple chain, work either of the **Loop Edgings** given on page 95.

EDALLIONS IN BABY IRISH CROCHET LACE

Victorian Leaf Medallion.

Ivy Leaf Medallion.

Materials: Silver Gauge Categories: 'Very Fine Yarns, Fine Yarns' for crocheting.
Silver Gauge Categories: 'Medium Fine, Medium' for padding.
Crochet hook sizes .60 mm – 2.50 mm.

Illustrations: Coats Mercer Crochet Nos 60 and 30 for crocheting.
Coats Mercer Crochet No 10 for padding.

Tensions: 7.5 cm (3 ins) square approximately. The tension may vary slightly with each medallion, but this will not affect the final garment.

The lace ground used to surround the medallions given here is always the **Double Picot Bar** (abbreviation: DPB) made as follows:

(8 ch, make a picot by inserting the hook through 6th ch from needle, yrh, draw through both loops on needle; 7 ch, make a second picot by inserting hook through 6th ch from needle, yrh, draw through both lops on hook; 2 ch.

Connect a DPB to an arc of previously made DPBs by working a dc over the chain space **between** the picots (abbreviated: dc over DPB).

NOTE: When working with the padding cord, work the 1st dc **only** over the fold, then work over all strands of padding cord.

Please see the **Crochet Techniques** section for details of any unfamiliar techniques.

Ivy Leaf Medallion:
Using the No 60 cotton for crocheting, and a 60 cm (24 ins) length of No 10 cotton for padding, fold the padding cord in half and 1 dc over the fold.

Round 1: (UCA, work 10 dc, turn;
 miss 2 dc, UC, 8 dc over next 8 dc)5.

Round 2: LC, yrh insert hook into bottom of first petal and draw through, (yrh, insert hook in bottom of next petal and draw through)4, yrh, draw through all loops on needle, turn.

Round 3: {Working up the side of a petal, ss into 1st dc, 1 dc in 2nd dc, (2 ch, miss 1 dc, 1 dc in next dc)3, 3 ch over point of petal and working down other side work 1 dc, (2 ch, miss 1 dc, 1 dc in next dc)3, ss opposite 1st ss, 1 tr between petals}5, ss into 1st ss.

Round 4: Cut 50 cm (20 ins) padding cord and fold in half; outline each petal thus:
 UC, (bring to correct side if necessary) and, working over **second** padding cord as well, 1 dc into side of petal, into fold of **second** cord and **over** first cord.
 Working over **both** cords, (2 dc into each 2 ch sp, 1 dc into each dc, 3 dc into 3 ch sp at tip of petal), TC to make petal stand out.
 LC, ss into first dc. Fasten off No 60 yarn.

Round 5: Using 30 cotton, 1 dc in edge of a petal, (DPB, miss approximately 9 dc, 1 dc in next dc)12, ss in 1st dc. (12 DPBs formed).

Round 6: Ss to centre of 1st DPB, *8 ch, dc over DPB, turn;
 9 dc over 8 ch sp, turn;
 1 dc in 1st dc, 1 tr in each of 8 dc, 1 dc in end of ch sp; (DPB, dc over DPB)2.
 Repeat from * to end of round, omit last dc on last repeat, ss into first dc.

Round 7: *DPB, 1 dc between 4th and 5th tr of Round 6, DPB, 1 dc into dc at end of tr group, (DPB, dc over DPB)2, DPB, 1 dc into 1st dc of tr group, repeat from * until the end of the round, ss into start of 1st DPB.

Round 8: Ss to centre of 1st DPB, *8 ch, dc over DPB, turn;
 9 dc over 8 ch sp, turn;
 1 dc in 1st dc, 1 tr in each of 8 dc, 1 dc in end of ch sp; (DPB, dc over DPB)4.
 Repeat from * to end of round, omit last dc on last repeat, ss into first dc. (4 tr groups and 16 DPBs altogether).

Round 9: *DPB, 1 dc between 4th and 5th tr of Round 8, (DPB, dc over DPB)4, DPB, dc into 1st dc; repeat from * to the end of the round. Ss into the start of 1st DPB. Fasten off.

Small Rose and Shells:
A group of (1 dc in next dc, 3 tr in next dc) is called a **shell**.

Work 4 ch with No 30 crocheting yarn, join with ss to form a ring.
Round 1: (1 dc, 3 ch)6; ss to 1st dc. (6 loops)
Round 2: (1 dc, 1 htr, 3 tr, 1 htr, 1 dc) into each ch sp; ss to 1st dc.
Round 3: (4 ch, dcb in next dc on Round 1)6.
Round 4: (1 dc, 1 htr, 4 tr, 1 htr, 1 dc) into each ch sp; ss into 1st dc.
Round 5: (4 ch, dcb into next dc on Round 3)6.
Round 6: (1 dc, 1 htr, 5 tr, 1 htr, 1 dc)6 into each ch sp; ss into 1st dc.
Round 7: (5 ch, dcb into next dc on Round 5)6.
Round 8: 1 dc in 1st ch sp, 12 ch, 1 dc into 2nd ch from hook, 1 dc into each ch, {1 ch, turn; 1 DC into each dc, 1 ch, turn, 1 DC in 1st dc, (3 tr in next dc, 1 dc into next dc)5, 1 dc into same ch sp on Round 7, 1 dc into next ch sp, 11 ch, flat join into central treble of 2nd shell from rose, 1 ch, 1 dc into each of next 11 ch)}4, 1 ch, turn, 1 DC in each dc, 1 ch, turn, 1 DC in 1st dc, (3 tr in next dc, 1 dc in next dc)3, 2 tr in next dc, 1 ss into 1st turning ch at beginning of round, 1 tr into same place as last tr, 1 DC in next dc, 3 tr in next dc, 1 dc in next dc, 1 dc in same ch sp on Round 7, 1 ss in 1st dc.
Fasten off.
Round 9: Join yarn to outside tip of a shell, working 1 dc into 1st dc; *8ch, 1 dc into central tr of 3rd shell, turn;
9 dc into ch sp, turn; 1 dc into 1st dc, 1 tr into each of next 8 dc, 1 dc into end of ch sp; DPB, 1 dc into tip of 1st shell on next arc, DPB, 1 dc into central tr of 3rd shell along, 8 ch, 1 dc into tip of 1st shell on next arc, turn;
9 dc into ch sp, turn;
1 dc into 1st dc, 1 tr in next 8 dc, 1 dc in end of ch sp, DPB, 1 dc into central tr of 3rd shell along, DPB*, 1 dc into tip of 1st shell of next arc, repeat from * to * once more. 1 ss into 1 dc at beginning of Round 9.
Round10: *DPB, 1 dc between 4th and 5th tr of Round 9, DPB, 1 dc into dc at end of tr group, (DPB, dc over DPB)2, DPB, 1 dc into 1st dc of tr group, repeat from * until the end of the round, ss into start of 1st DPB.
Round11: Ss to centre of 1st DPB, *8 ch, dc over DPB, turn;
9 dc over 8 ch sp, turn;
1 dc in 1st dc, 1 tr in each of 8 dc, 1 dc in end of ch sp; (DPB, dc over DPB)4. Repeat from * to end of round, omit last dc on last repeat, ss into first dc. (4 tr groups and 16 DPBs altogether).
Round12: *DPB, 1 dc between 4th and 5th tr of Round 11, (DPB, dc over DPB)4, DPB, dc into 1st dc; repeat from * to the end of the round. Ss into the start of 1st DPB. Fasten off.

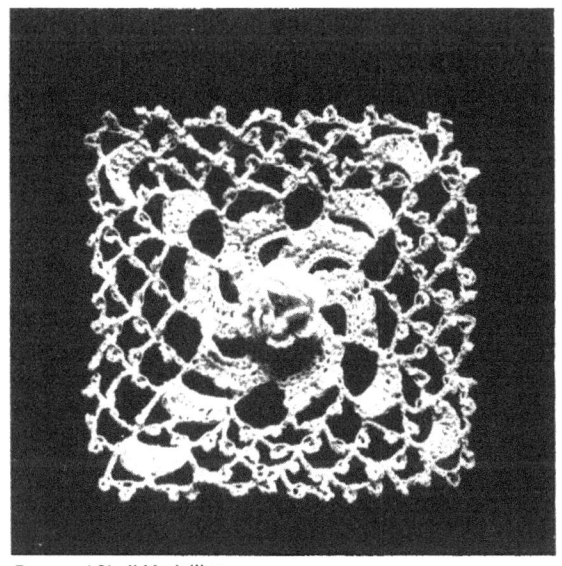
Rose and Shell Medallion.

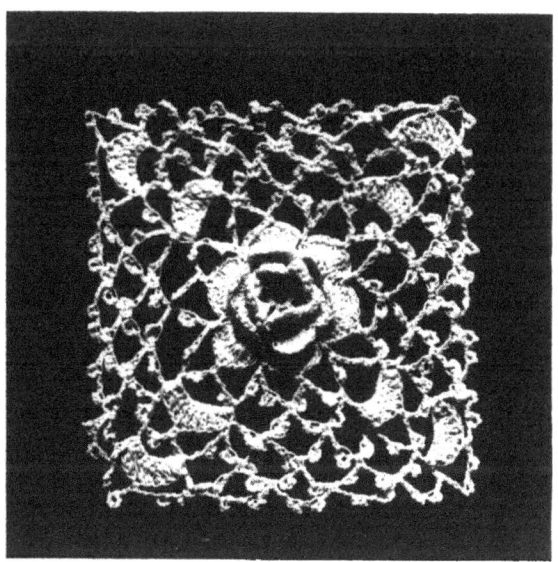
Basic Square with Rose Centre.

Basic Square with Rose Centre:

Work 8 ch; join with ss into a ring.

Round 1: (1 dc, 5 ch)6 into ring, ss into 1st dc to join.
Round 2: (1 dc, 6 tr, 1 dc) into each ch sp; ss into 1st dc.
Round 3: (7 ch, 1 dcb into next dc of Round 1)6. (6 loops made.)
Round 4: (1 dc, 8 tr, 1 dc)6; ss into 1st dc to join.
Round 5: (8 ch, 1 dcb into 1st dc of Round 3)6.
Round 6: (1 dc, 10 tr, 1 dc)6; ss into 1st dc to join.
Round 7: (DPB, 1 dc into top of 5th tr in next petal, DPB, 1 dc between petals)6; there will be 12 double picot bars worked evenly round the rose.
Round 8: Ss to centre of 1st DPB, *8 ch, dc over DPB, turn;
9 dc over 8 ch sp, turn;
1 dc in 1st dc, 1 tr in each of 8 dc, 1 dc in end of ch sp; (DPB, dc over DPB)2. Repeat from * to end of round, omit last dc on last repeat, ss into 1st dc.
Round 9: *DPB, 1 dc between 4th and 5th tr of Round 8, DPB, 1 dc into dc at end of tr group, (DPB, dc over DPB)2, DPB, 1 dc into 1st dc of tr group, repeat from * until the end of the round, ss into start of 1st DPB.
Round 10: Ss to centre of 1st DPB, *8 ch, dc over DPB, turn;
9 dc over 8 ch sp, turn;
1 dc in 1st dc, 1 tr in each of 8 dc, 1 dc in end of ch sp; (DPB, dc over DPB)4. Repeat from * to end of round, omit last dc on last repeat, ss into first dc. (4 tr groups and 16 DPBs altogether).
Round 11: *DPB, 1 dc between 4th and 5th tr of Round 10, (DPB, dc over DPB)4, DPB, dc into 1st dc; repeat from * to the end of the round. Ss into the start of 1st DPB. Fasten off.

Half Shamrock Medallion:

Working in No 30 yarn, make (16 ch, 1 dc in 1st ch made)2.

Round 1: Working over chain spaces and the doubled padding cord, work 27 dc into each ch sp and TC each time. (2 petals.)

Round 2: LC, dc into each dc, ss into 1st dc.

Round 3: Ss into next 3 dc, {1 dc into next dc, (DPB, miss 4 dc, 1 dc in next dc)3, DPB, miss 8 dc}2, ss in 1st dc. (9 loops in all.)

Round 4: Ss to centre of 1st DPB, *8 ch, dc over DPB, turn;
9 dc over 8 ch sp, turn;
1 dc in 1st dc, 1 tr in each of 8 dc, 1 dc ino end of ch sp; (DPB, dc over DPB)2. Repeat from * to end of round, omit last dc on last repeat, ss into first dc.

Round 5: *DPB, 1 dc between 4th and 5th tr of Round 4, DPB, 1 dc into dc at end of tr group, (DPB, dc over DPB)2, DPB, 1 dc into 1st dc of tr group, repeat from * until the end of the round, ss into start of 1st DPB.

Round 6: Ss to centre of 1st DPB, *8 ch, dc over DPB, turn;
9 dc over 8 ch sp, turn;
1 dc in 1st dc, 1 tr in each of 8 dc, 1 dc in end of ch sp; (DPB, dc over DPB)4. Repeat from * to end of round, omit last dc on last repeat, ss into first dc.

Round 7: *DPB, 1 dc between 4th and 5th tr of Round 6, (DPB, dc over DPB)4, DPB, dc into 1st dc; repeat from * to the end of the round. Ss into the start of 1st DPB. Fasten off.

Daisy Medallion:

Work 8 ch using No 30 cotton; join with ss to form a ring.

Round 1: Work 16 dc into ring; ss to 1st dc to join.

Round 2: (2 dc in next dc, 1 dc in next dc)8; ss to 1st dc.

Round 3: (11 ch, 1 ss in next dc)23, 5 ch, 1 dtr in same place as last ss. (24 loops).

Round 4: 1 dcj over 1st 2 loops, *(8 ch, 1 dcj over next 2 loops, 1 ch, turn;
9 dc into ch sp, turn;
1 dc into 1st dc, 8 tr in next dc, 1 dc in end of ch sp, {8 ch, (DPB, 1 jdc in next 2 ch sp petals)2}; repeat from * until end of round, omit last dcj, ss into 1st dc. 4 tr groups and 8 DPBs.)

Round 5: *DPB, 1 dc between 4th and 5th tr of Round 4, DPB, 1 dc into dc at end of tr group, (DPB, dc over DPB)2, DPB, 1 dc into 1st dc of tr group, repeat from * until the end of the round, ss into start of 1st DPB.

Round 6: Ss to centre of 1st DPB, *8 ch, dc over DPB, turn;
9 dc over 8 ch sp, turn;
1 dc in 1st dc, 1 tr in each of 8 dc, 1 dc in end of ch sp; (DPB, dc over DPB)4. Repeat from * to end of round, omit last dc on last repeat, ss into first dc. (4 tr groups and 16 DPBs altogether).

Round 7: *DPB, 1 dc between 4th and 5th tr of Round 6, (DPB, dc over DPB)4, DPB, dc into 1st dc; repeat from * to the end of the round. Ss into the start of 1st DPB. Fasten off.

Daisy Medallion.

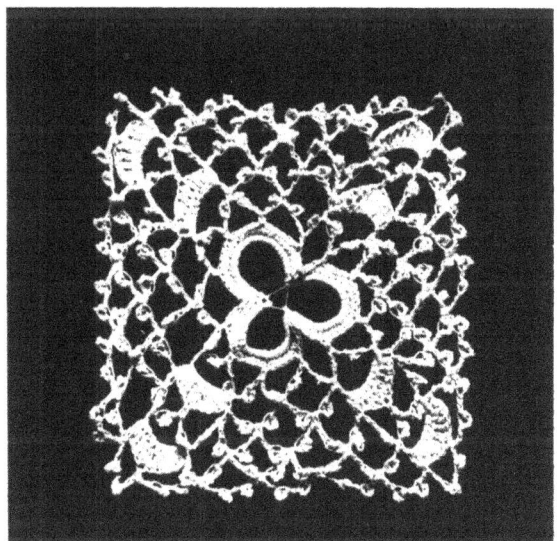

Basic Square with Shamrock Centre.

Basic Square with Shamrock Centre:
Working in No 30 yarn, make 16 ch, 1 dc in 1st ch made; (15 ch, 1 dc in 1st ch made)2.
Using a 36 cm (14 ins) strand of No 10 cotton folded in half:

Round 1: Working over chain spaces and the doubled padding cord, UC, 25 dc into each ch sp and TC each time.

Round 2: LC, dc into each dc, ss into 1st dc.

Round 3: Ss into next 3 dc, {1 dc into next dc, (DPB, miss 4 dc, 1 dc in next dc)3, DPB, miss 8 dc}3, ss in 1st dc. (3 loops to a petal, 1 between; 12 loops in all.)

Round 4: Ss to centre of 1st DPB, *8 ch, dc over DPB, turn;
9 dc over 8 ch sp, turn;
1 dc in 1st dc, 1 tr in each of 8 dc, 1 dc in end of ch sp; (DPB, dc over DPB)2. Repeat from * to end of round, omit last dc on last repeat, ss into first dc.

Round 5: *DPB, 1 dc between 4th and 5th tr of Round 4, DPB, 1 dc into dc at end of tr group, (DPB, dc over DPB)2, DPB, 1 dc into 1st dc of tr group, repeat from * until the end of the round, ss into start of 1st DPB.

Round 6: Ss to centre of 1st DPB, *8 ch, dc over DPB, turn;
9 dc over 8 ch sp, turn;
1 dc in 1st dc, 1 tr in each of 8 dc, 1 dc into end of ch sp; (DPB, dc over DPB)4. Repeat from * to end of round, omit last dc on last repeat, ss into first dc. (4 tr groups and 16 DPBs altogether).

Round 7: *DPB, 1 dc between 4th and 5th tr of Round 6, (DPB, dc over DPB)4, DPB, dc into 1st dc; repeat from * to the end of the round. Ss into the start of 1st DPB. Fasten off.

Wheel Medallion:

Using No 30 yarn, wind yarn round index finger 12 times; remove wound yarn with care.

Round 1: 36 dc over the foundation ring; ss to 1st dc.

Round 2: (9 ch, miss 5 dc, dc into next dc)6; ss into 1st ch.

Round 3: (12 dc over next 9 ch sp)6; ss into 1st dc.

Round 4: 3 ch, 1 tr in each dc of Round 3, ss to 3rd ch.

Round 5: 1 dc, *8 ch, miss 5 tr, 1 dc, turn;
9 dc over 8 ch sp, turn;
1 dc in 1st dc, 1 tr in each of 8 dc, 1 dc in end of ch sp; (DPB, miss 5 tr, 1 dc)2. Repeat from * to end of round, omit last dc on last repeat, ss into first dc.

Round 6: *DPB, 1 dc between 4th and 5th tr of Round 5, DPB, 1 dc into dc at end of tr group, (DPB, dc over DPB)2, DPB, 1 dc into 1st dc of tr group, repeat from * until the end of the round, ss into start of 1st DPB.

Round 7: Ss to centre of 1st DPB, *8 ch, dc over DPB, turn;
9 dc over 8 ch sp, turn;
1 dc in 1st dc, 1 tr in each of 8 dc, 1 dc in end of ch sp; (DPB, dc over DPB)4. Repeat from * to end of round, omit last dc on last repeat, ss into first dc. (4 tr groups and 16 DPBs altogether).

Round 8: *DPB, 1 dc between 4th and 5th tr of Round 7, (DPB, dc over DPB)4, DPB, dc into 1st dc; repeat from * to the end of the round. Ss into the start of 1st DPB. Fasten off.

Wheel Medallion.

Cobweb Medallion.

Cobweb Medallion: (P = 6 chain picot.)

Using No 30 yarn work 30 ch, 1 ss into 30th ch from needle, work another 30 ch, 1 ss into same 30th ch as before. Overlap the 2 rings.

Round 1: Work 36 dc into doubled rings, 1 ss to 1st dc, 2 turning ch, 1 dc in next dc, P, (1 dc in next 3 dc, P)11, 1 dc in next dc, 1 ss in 1st dc. (12 picots.)

Round 2: *DPB, 1 dc in centre dc between next picots, repeat from * round ring, 1 ss in 1st ch of 1st DPB, turn.

Round 3: Ss to centre of 1st DPB, *8 ch, dc over DPB, turn;
9 dc over 8 ch sp, turn;
1 dc in 1st dc, 1 tr in each of 8 dc, 1 dc in end of ch sp; (DPB, dc over DPB)2. Repeat from * to end of round, omit last dc on last repeat, ss into first dc.

Round 4: *DPB, 1 dc between 4th and 5th tr of Round 3, DPB, 1 dc into dc at end of tr group, (DPB, dc over DPB)2, DPB, 1 dc into 1st dc of tr group, repeat from * until the end of the round, ss into start of 1st DPB.

Round 5: Ss to centre of 1st DPB, *8 ch, dc over DPB, turn;
9 dc over 8 ch sp, turn;
1 dc in 1st dc, 1 tr in each of 8 dc, 1 dc in end of ch sp; (DPB, dc over DPB)4. Repeat from * to end of round, omit last dc on last repeat, ss into first dc. (4 tr groups and 16 DPBs altogether).

Round 6: *DPB, 1 dc between 4th and 5th tr of Round 5, (DPB, dc over DPB)4, DPB, dc into 1st dc; repeat from * to the end of the round. Ss into the start of 1st DPB. Fasten off.

Cobweb:

Secure medallion to a firm foundation. Thread a needle with No 60 yarn, attach yarn on wrong side of work to a dc. Fill the ring with yarn by working from 1 to 17 on the chart, *crossing from 1 to 2, then skipping 2 or 3 dc from 2 to 3 and so on from *.

Take the yarn to the centre, wind the yarn round the threads to hold them together, then weave the yarn over and under, round and round, until a web has been formed. Do not worry too much about absolute symmetry. Fasten off.

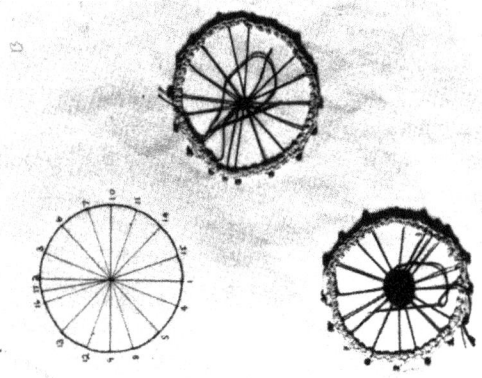

Stages in working the centre of a Cobweb Motif.

Victorian Leaf Medallion:
Round 1: Cut 60 cm (24 ins) No 10 yarn and use as a padding cord. Fold in half and, using No 60 yarn, 1 dc into fold. UCA, 14 dc, turn; (1st leaf tip)
LC, 1 ch, UC, 1 DC in each dc down LHS, 3 DC in base of leaf, 10 DC up RHS, UCA, 3 dc, LC, 1 ch, turn; (2nd leaf tip)
UC, 1 DC in each of 3 dc just made, 1 DC into each RHS st, 3 DC into the base, 1 DC up LHS excluding the last 3 sts, UCA, 3 dc, LC, 1 ch, turn; (3rd leaf tip)
UC, 1 DC into 3 dc just made, 1 DC into each LHS st to base, 3 DC into base, 1 DC into each RHS st excluding the last 6 sts, UCA, 3 dc, LC, 1 ch, turn; (4th leaf tip)
UC, 3 DC into 3 dc just made, 1 DC into each RHS st, 3 DC into base, 1 DC into each LHS st, excluding last 6 sts, UCA, 3 dc, LC, 1 ch, turn; (5th leaf tip)
UC, 1 DC into each LHS st to base, 3 DC in base, 1 DC in each RHS st excluding last 6 sts, UCA, 3 dc, LC, 1 ch, turn; (6th leaf tip)
UC, 1 DC in last 3 dc made, 1 DC in each RHS st to base, 3 DC in base, 1 DC in each LHS st excluding last 6 sts, UCA, 3 dc, LC, 1 ch, turn; (7th leaf tip)
1 DC in each of 3 dc just made, 1 DC in each RHS st to base, 1 DC in base, UCA, 5 dc, miss 2 dc on base of leaf, ss in next dc. Fasten off.
Round 2: Using No 30 yarn, attach to central leaf tip made, (DPB, 1 dc in next leaf tip)3, (DPB, leave space, 1 dc)6 evenly to next leaf tip, (DPB, 1 dc in next leaf tip)3, ss to central leaf tip. (12 DPBs made.)
Round 3: Ss to centre of 1st DPB, *8 ch, dc over DPB, turn;
9 dc over 8 ch sp, turn;
1 dc in 1st dc, 1 tr in each of 8 dc, 1 dc in end of ch sp; (DPB, dc over DPB)2. Repeat from * to end of round, omit last dc on last repeat, ss into first dc.
Round 4: *DPB, 1 dc between 4th and 5th tr of Round 3, DPB, 1 dc into dc at end of tr group, (DPB, dc over DPB)2, DPB, 1 dc into 1st dc of tr group, repeat from * until the end of the round, ss into start of 1st DPB.
Round 5: Ss to centre of 1st DPB, *8 ch, dc over DPB, turn;
9 dc over 8 ch sp, turn;
1 dc in 1st dc, 1 tr in each of 8 dc, 1 dc in end of ch sp; (DPB, dc over DPB)4. Repeat from * to end of round, omit last dc on last repeat, ss into first dc. (4 tr groups and 16 DPBs altogether).
Round 6: *DPB, 1 dc between 4th and 5th tr of Round 5, (DPB, dc over DPB)4, DPB, dc into 1st dc; repeat from * to the end of the round. Ss into the start of 1st DPB. Fasten off.

CHRISTENING APRON

Materials:	Silver Gauge Categories: 'Very Fine Yarns', 'Fine Yarns'. Silver Gauge Category: 'Medium Fine Yarns' for padding. Crochet hook sizes .60 mm – 1.50 mm.
Illustration:	20g balls of Coats Mercer Crochet, all in the same shade: One ball No 60; five balls No 30; one ball No 10. Steel crochet hook size .75 mm. 2.5 m (8 ft) of 4 cm (1.5 ins) wide ribbon.
Tension:	Skirt length: 47 cm (18.5 ins), but this will lengthen after a time. Bodice top across: 10.5 cm (4.25 ins).

This enchanting little **Christening Apron** is not too difficult to make, and could well become a cherished heirloom in the family. The apron can be tacked over any plain christening dress pattern; white over cream, or cream over white, makes an attractive combination. Even a plain, long nightgown can be turned into a garment fit for a special occasion when this little gem is tucked away in your drawer.

Dahlia:
Tension: 5 cm diameter.

Using No 60 cotton, make 10 ch and join with ss into a ring.
Round 1: 24 dc into ring, ss to join.
Round 2: *14 ch, 1 dc in 2nd ch from hook, 1 dc in each ch, 1 ss into corresponding dc on ring, ss into **front** loop of next (2nd) dc on **ring**, turn;
1 dc into each of next 13 dc on the petal, turn with 1 ch, miss 1st dc, 1 dc into each dc, ss into **front** loop of second dc on the ring, ss into front loop of next dc (one petal made). Repeat from * until there are 12 petals. (Note: each petal has been worked over 2 dc).

Make 2 more flowers, this time starting Round 2 with 12 and 10 chains respectively, so making shorter petals.

Sew the three Dahlia flowers together; use a tapestry needle threaded with the No 60 yarn and connect the flowers together through the rings using small, unobtrusive stitches.

Background Lace:
Double Picot Bar (abbreviated DPB): 8 ch, 1 ss into 6th ch from hook, 7 ch, 1 ss into 6th ch from hook, 2 ch, 1 DC in next dc.

Using No 30 cotton, SS to join into a dc on Round 2 of the Dahlia.
Round 1: 4 DPB, {1 DPB, (DC into every alternate dc)}4, 4 DPB, {1 DPB, (DC into every alternate dc)}4. (16 DPBs in all.)
Round 2: Ss into centre of next DPB, turn;
1 DPB, 1 dc over centre of next DPB of last round.
Round 3: Ss into centre of next DPB, turn;
1 DPB, 1 dc over centre of next DPB of last round.
Round 4: Ss into centre of next DPB, turn;
1 DPB, 1 dc over centre of next DPB of last round.
Round 5: Ss into centre of next DPB, turn;
1 DPB, 1 dc over centre of next DPB of last round.
Round 6: Ss to centre of next DPB, *8 ch, 1 dc into centre of next DPB, turn;
9 dc over the 8 ch, turn;
1 dc in 1st dc, 8 tr in each of next 8 dc, 1 dc in end of ch sp, (1 DPB, 1 dc over centre of next DPB)2. Repeat from * to end of Round 6, ss in 1st dc.

Round 7: *1 DPB, 1 dc between 4th and 5th tr, 1 DPB, 1 dc in dc at end of treble group, (1 DPB, 1 dc over centre of next DPB)2, 1 DPB, 1 dc in 1st dc of treble group, repeat from * to end of Round 7, ss into 1st ch of first DPB.

Round 8: Ss to centre of 1st DPB. *4 ch, 1 dc over centre of next DPB* to end of Round 8, but working 8 ch instead of 4 ch into each corner. This forms a **straight** edge to outline the dahlia medallion.

Round 9: Using No 60 cotton, and 140 cm (55 ins) No 10 padding cotton 4-fold by folding in half, and then in half again, dc over padding fold **and** over 4 ch sp, UC, 3 dc, *4 dc in next 4 ch sp* around the medallion, working 8 dc into each 8 ch sp, ss in 1st dc.

Round 10: *1 dc, 2 ch in every alternate dc round medallion*, ss in 1st dc, ss in 1st sp.

Round 11: LC, *2 dc, 2 ch into every ch sp*, ss in 1st of 2 dc, turn;

Round 12: *2 dc, 2 ch into every ch sp*, working (2 dc, 2 ch, 2 dc) into corner 2 ch sps.

Bodice Edging:

Outline the bodice loosely with No 10 cotton and measure out 3 more lengths + 10 cm (4 ins). Fold and fold in half again, making a 4-fold padding cord.

Row 1: 1 dc over fold **and** over 2 ch sp of Round 12, UC, dc over same 2 ch sp, (2 dc over next 2 ch sp)5, 1 dc in next 2 ch sp (13 dc altogether), **LC, turn;

Row 2: 7 ch, miss 5 dc, 1 dc in next dc, 7 ch, miss 5 dc, 1 dc in next dc, turn;

Row 3: 4 dc in 1st ch sp, 4 ch, 6 dc in same ch sp, 3 dc in next ch sp, 7 ch, turn;

Row 4: miss 6 dc, 1 dc in next dc, turn;

Row 5: 5 dc, 4 ch, 5 dc in 7 ch sp; 2 dc, 4 ch, 4 dc in rest of 7 ch sp, turn;

Row 6: *UC, 1 dc in same 2 ch sp as last dc worked on previous row, 2 dc over next 2 ch sps (as before) for 12 dcs, repeat from ** to *; UC, ***2 dc over next 2 ch sps for 12 dcs, 1 dc into next 2 ch sp; repeat from ** to *, UC, 1 dc in same 2 ch sp as last dc worked of previous 13 dc, 2 dc over next 2 ch sp as before for 12 dc, repeat from ** to * again.***

*** to *** forms the edging pattern; work this around the whole medallion, ss into 1st dc of edging. Fasten off.

Skirt Pattern:

Work the following 36 medallions:

3 Rose Medallions (R)
3 Rose Shell Medallions (R/S)
3 Ivy Leaf Medallions (I/L)
18 Shamrock Medallions (S)

3 Cobweb Medallions (C)
3 Daisy Medallions (D)
3 Victorian Leaf Medallions (V/L)

Arrange them as shown on the chart, and connect them invisibly as follows, starting at the arrow:

Using No 30 cotton, start with a dc into the top right hand corner DPB of the second medallion down.

*8 ch, 1 ss into 6th ch from hook, 2 ch, 1 dc into corresponding DPB of medallion above, 8 ch, 1 ss into 6th ch from hook, 2 ch, 1 dc into next DPB on medallion below, repeat from * to the end of each medallion, and continue joining the next pair of medallions in the same way along the row. Make invisible horizontal seams along the rest of the rows. Fasten off.

**Start with a dc into the corner picot of the third medallion down on the right hand side. Work from * to ** once more. Work the other vertical seams in the same way.

Christening Apron chart.

\multicolumn{6}{c}{DAHLIA}
C	S	C	S	C	S
S	R	S	R	S	R
R/S	S	R/S	S	R/S	S
S	D	S	D	S	D
I/L	S	I/L	S	I/L	S
S	V/L	S	V/L	S	V/L

Gathering the Skirt Top:

Row 1: Work 1 dc into the top DPB of the medallion at the top right hand side of the skirt. Along the top of the skirt work *8ch, 1 ss into 6th ch from hook, 2 ch, 1 dc into next DPB along*. Repeat instructions to the end of the row, turn.

Row 2: Ss into centre of 1st DPB, repeat from * to * the end of the row, turn and ss into centre of first DPB.

Row 3: Repeat from * to * to the end of the row, turn, ss into 1st picot.

Row 4: Gather the top by working a dc into the top corner picot and a dc into all the other picots along the row to the end. Fasten off.

Joining the Bodice:

Sew the bodice onto the skirt, matching centre fronts and arranging the scallops to overlap the outside of the skirt. Gather the remaining top edges of the skirt either side of the bodice to 4 cms in width.

Working the Skirt Edging:

Row 1: Using No 60, straighten the edges of the skirt, work 1 dc into the corner DPB at the top left hand side medallion. Work down skirt side as follows:
*4 ch, 1 dc into next DPB, repeat from * to the bottom of the skirt. If the edging appears too tight, simply replace the 4 ch with 5 ch or 6 ch. Now work 8 ch, 1 dc into the corner DPB, 6 ch, 1 dc into the pLs along the bottom of the skirt, 8 ch, 1 dc into the corner DPB and 4 ch, 1 dc into the PLs up the other side of the skirt to the last DPB.

Cut a length of No 10 cotton to fit round the 3 sides of the skirt 4 times. Fold it in half, then fold it in half again, ending up with a 4-fold padding cord.

Row 2: 1 dc over the fold of the padding cord and into top corner of the skirt where last dc of previous row was worked. Work round 3 sides of skirt: UC, 4 dc into 4 ch sp, 8 dc into 8 ch sp at the corner, 6 dc over 6 ch sps along the bottom of the skirt, 8 dc over the 8 ch sp at the corner, 4 dc over each of the remaining 4 ch sps to the end, 1 ch, LC, turn.
Fasten off the padding cord to hold it firm.

Row 3: *2 ch, 1 dc into every alternate dc around the skirt*, 1 dc in last st, turn;

Row 4: 2 ch, 2 dc in next 2 ch sp, *2 ch, 2 dc in next 2 ch sp, repeat from * round skirt edges, ending with a dc in last st, 1 ch, turn.

Skirt Edging Pattern:

Work the skirt edging in the same way as the bodice edging, omitting the padding cord throughout:

Row 1: 2 dc into the 1st 2 ch sp, 2 dc into each of next 2 ch sps, until 12 dc have been worked, 1 dc into next 2 ch sp (13 dc altogether), turn;

Row 2: **7 ch, miss 5 dc, 1 dc in next dc, 7 ch, miss 5 dc, 1 dc in next dc, turn;

Row 3: 4 dc in 1st ch sp, 4 ch, 6 dc in same ch sp, 3 dc in next ch sp, 7 ch, turn;

Row 4: miss 6 dc, 1 dc in next dc, turn;

Row 5: 5 dc, 4 ch, 5 dc in 7 ch sp; 2 dc, 4 ch, 4 dc in rest of 7 ch sp, turn;

Row 6: *1 dc in same 2 ch sp as last dc worked on previous row, 2 dc over next 2 ch sps (as before) for 12 dcs, repeat from ** to *; UC, ***2 dc over next 2 ch sps for 12 dc, 1 dc into next 2 ch sp; repeat from ** to *, 1 dc in same 2 ch sp as last dc worked of previous 13 dc, 2 dc over next 2 ch sp as before for 12 dc, repeat from ** to * again.***
*** to *** forms the edging pattern; work this around the whole medallion, ss into 1st dc of edging. Fasten off.

Sew the ribbon along the top of the skirt and up the side of the bodice. The ribbon is tied around the waist at the back. The ribbon over the shoulders is sewn at the back onto the waist band so that it forms braces.

The inner rows of the flower petals on the bodice have been sewn onto the background lace as have most but not all of the other petals on the other two rounds. Some of the petals have been twisted once and then sewn down for a naturalistic look.

olero

![bolero photograph]

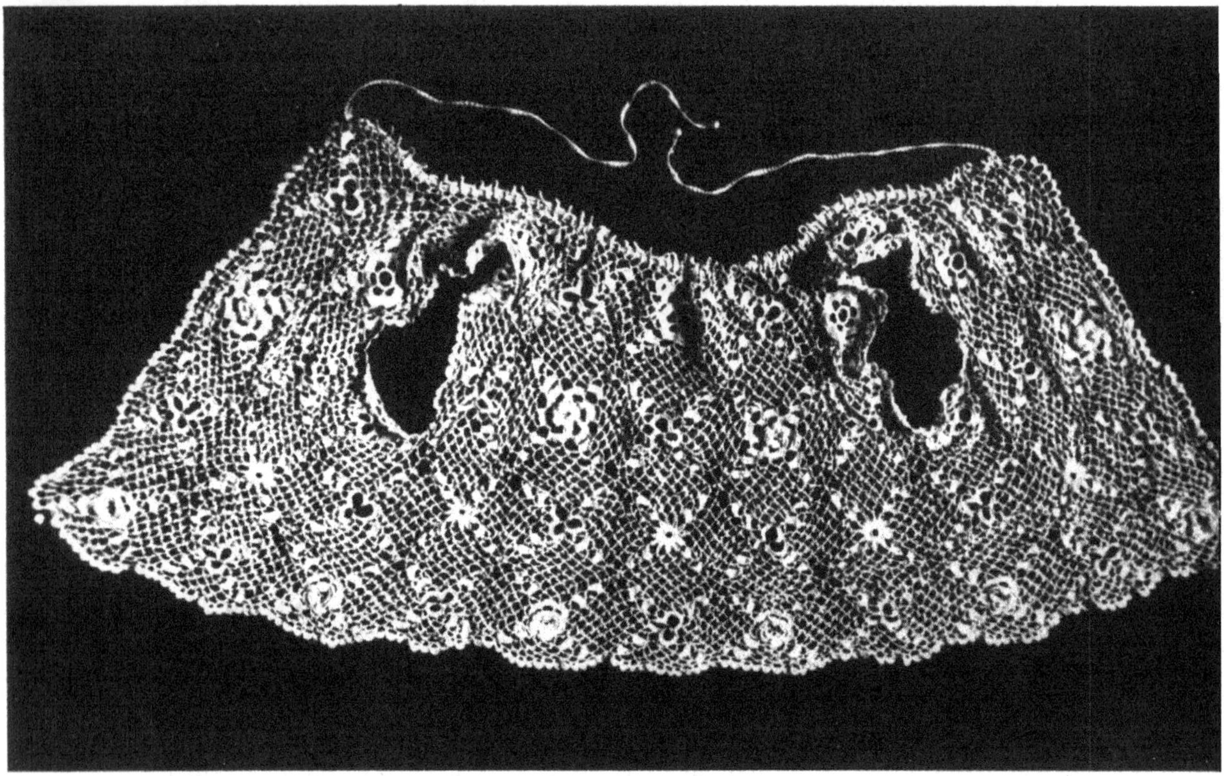

Materials:	Silver Gauge Categories: 'Very Fine Yarns' for crocheting; Silver Gauge Category: 'Medium Fine Yarns' for padding. Crochet hook sizes .75 mm – 1.75 mm.
Illustration:	20 g balls of Coats Mercer Crochet in the same shade: Six balls No 40; one ball No 10. 1.25 mm steel crochet hook.
Tension:	Approximately 8 cm (3.25 ins) square for each medallion. To fit bust 81 – 91 cms (32 – 36 ins).

This bolero is a delightful, and very versatile, addition to a wardrobe. Make it in a pastel shade and wear it over dark taffeta or velvet for a very striking effect. The illustrated version was made using the medallions listed below, but the whole garment could be made using only the **Shamrock** and one flower medallion if any of the other patterns seem too difficult at first.

The basic medallion patterns are used to make the bolero but the No 30 cotton is replaced by No 40 cotton, though the hook size used for the work is larger. This results in finer, but larger, medallions.

Work the following medallions:

    2 Shamrock Halves (S/H)   6 Rose Medallions (R)
    5 Daisy Medallions (D)   4 Rose Shell Medallions (R/S)
    22 Shamrock Medallions (S)   5 Wheel Medallions (W)

Assembly:

Arrange the medallions as shown on the chart, and assemble them as detailed below, making sure you allow openings for the armholes.

Horizontal Joins:

Start with a dc into the top right hand corner DPB of the bottom medallion (arrow 1): *8 ch, 1 ss into 6th ch from hook, 2 ch, 1 dc into corresponding DPB of the motif above, 8 ch, 1 ss into 6th ch from hook, 2 ch, 1 dc into next DPB on the bottom motif once more, repeat from * to the end of each medallion pair, then continue joining corresponding medallions to the end of the row. Fasten off**.

Rejoin yarn for the next joining row, starting with a dc into the corner DPB of the 2nd medallion up on the right hand side (arrow 2) and work again from * to **. Continue joining horizontal seams in this way.

Vertical Joins:

Turn the work so that the vertical rows are horizontal. Now join these rows in exactly the same way as the horizontal rows, starting with a dc into the top right hand corner DPB (arrow 3). Work from * to ** to arrow 4 and fasten off.

Rejoin yarn at arrow 5 and repeat to arrow 6; fasten off. Work all the other joins in the same way.

Join the side seams in the same way, allowing space for the armholes.

R	S	R	R	S	R
S	D	S	S	D	S
H/S	S	R/S	R/S	S	H/S
	W	S	S	W	
	S	NECK OPENING		S	
	W	S	W	S	W
	S	R/S	S	R/S	S
D	S	D	S	D	
S	R	S	R	S	

Edging Patterns:

Lower Border Edging:
Row 1: Starting at bottom left hand corner, join with dc into picot, *4 ch, 1 dc into next picot* all round out edge of garment. Ss into 1st dc.
Row 2: **(1 dc, 1 htr, 2 tr, 1 dtr, 2 tr, 1 htr, 1 dc) into each 4 ch sp on bottom edge.
Row 3: Up **front edge:** 7 ch, *miss 4 ch, 1 tr in next dc, 4 ch* to top corner, turn; (1 dc, 1 htr, 2 tr, 1 dtr, 2 tr, 1 htr, 1 dc) into each 4 ch sp to the top.
Repeat Row 3 for the other front edge of the bolero, **matching** squares.

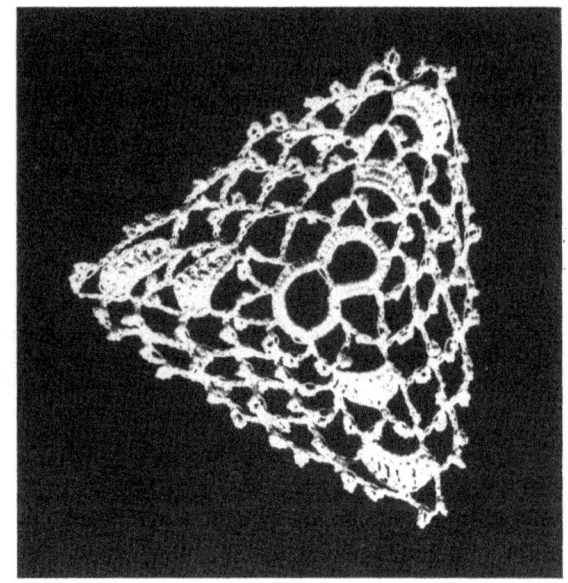

Half-Shamrock Medallion.

Armhole Edgings:
The armhole edgings are worked in exactly the same way as the bottom edge of the bolero.

Hoop Border for Neck Edging (Multiple of 3 + 1 {1 tr, 2 ch, miss 2 ch} band):
Start with right side facing you.
Use 418 cm (165 ins) No 10 folded in half, and folded in half again, as a padding cord.

Row 1: Join yarn to 1st of the 4 ch of the first sp on the neck edge, 5 ch, *1 tr in centre of 4 ch sp, 2 ch, 1 tr in dc between this and next 4 ch sp, 2 ch*. Repeat from * to * omitting last 2 ch.
Row 2: Ss in 1st 2 ch sp. UCA, 1 dc in fold of cord, UC, 1 dc in 1st 2 ch sp, *2 dc in each of next 2 ch sps, 1 dc in next 2 ch sp, UCA, 10 dc, UC, 1 dc in same 2 ch sp of garment*. Fasten off.

Cord Tie:

A cord can conveniently be threaded in and out of the first row of the **Hoop Border** to gather the edging to the desired neckline.
Cord 1: Work a 128 cm (50 ins) foundation chain in No 10 cotton. Turn and dc to end.
Cord 2: Work a 128 cm (50 ins) foundation chain in No 10 cotton, dc over this as though it were a padding cord.
Cord 3: Make a 128 cm (50 ins) long double crochet chain. (See **Crochet Techniques**.)

Soak the bolero to shrink it. Pull it into shape whilst still wet and dry flat.

Techniques

The basic stitches of Irish Crochet are exactly the same as those used for short hook crochet. These are described below to remind readers who have only a slight knowledge of crochet, and to start off those who have not yet attempted it. These basic stitches are very simple indeed, and anyone who can knit is certainly capable of making basic Irish Crochet. The few unusual techniques needed are also described.

The main difference between Irish and ordinary short hook crochet lies in the difference of approach. Short hook crochet is worked on the flat, backwards and forwards, to form a rectangular or shaped fabric piece, or it is worked in the round to form a tube or a medallion. Both methods often involve keeping careful count of stitches, which many people find very demanding.

Irish Crochet, on the other hand, is a rather easy-going form of needlecrafting. It depends, essentially, on making one or more motifs, chosen from simple basic shapes or from rather more elaborate ones. The individual motifs, often assembled into sprigs, may be sewn **onto** a lace ground or, more subtly, connected **with** a crochet lace or just a few crochet bars. The designs need not be symmetrical, the motifs need not be identical, the connecting lace is worked in a way which is immediately pleasing to the worker rather than in a set pattern. The whole project takes on a unique, individual and 'free' approach which can be used quite easily for one of the most enjoyable forms of lacemaking.

An important feature of much Irish Crochet Lace is that basic stitches are, in part, worked over padding. This allows sections of the design a greater relief structure than ordinary crochet can provide. Consequently it is often not even necessary to start the work with a foundation chain - double crochet, occasionally treble crochet, worked over the padding yarn can form the foundation for the work.

Yet another feature of Irish Crochet is that some of the more elaborate motifs, predominantly the larger flower motifs, are made with overlapping pieces to give a truly three dimensional look to these motifs. Detailed directions are given in the first few patterns for those who have not worked in this way before; again, the actual working of the stitches is as simple as the basic crochet stitches, it is only the method of using them which is different.

A few quite new suggestions, making use of a modern technology not available to the old workers, are given here for the first time. They can help you overcome some of the common stumbling blocks for beginners. Very few directions for Irish Crochet, old or new, give more than the motif instructions together with a brief indication of how to work the filling. Detailed filling directions are provided under **Lacemaking Methods.**

As in every worthwhile craft which may, on occasion, be lifted to the status of an artform, you will find yourself inventing methods of your own. These new ideas, and the ways of carrying them out, can lift your work into the highest plane, and give you that special thrill that only truly creative work can give. Don't be afraid to try out your own techniques, just because they are not given here!

CROCHET TECHNIQUES CONTENTS

	Page
Basic Crocheting:	
Threading the Yarn	70
Slip Knot and First Loop	70
Chain Stitch	71
Foundation Chain	71
Starting and Turning Chains	71
Slip Stitch (ss, SS)	72
Double Crochet (dc, DC)	72
Half Treble (htr, HTR)	73
Treble (tr, TR)	73
Double Treble (dtr, DTR)	73
Triple Treble (tr tr, TR TR)	73
Double Crochet Chain	74
Crocheting into the Back (dcb)	74
Crochet Ornaments:	
Chain Picot	75
Left to Right Chain Picot	75
Clones Knot	76
Crocheting with Padding:	
Crocheting over Foundation Chains	77
Double Crocheting over Padding	77
Bosses	77
Use Cord Alone	78
Use Cord	78
Leave Cord	78
Tighten Cord	78
Joins:	
Joining Chains into Rings	79
Joining Rounds	79
Joining Motifs	79
Double Crochet Join (dcj)	79
Miscellaneous Techniques:	
Simple Increases	80
Avoiding Cutting Yarn	80
Shaping Rings and Coils	80
Fastening Off:	80

BASIC CROCHETING

The **basic** short hook crochet stitch, the basis of all the other stitches, is a loop of yarn drawn (pulled) through another loop by means of the hook at the end of the short hook crochet needle. The new loop may simply be drawn through a loop or loops already on the needle, or the hook may be inserted into a previously made stitch before the yarn is drawn through one, some or all of the loops on the needle (see below for details).

Start by putting a slip knot on the needle (see below). The crochet needle is held in the **right** hand by right-handed crocheters. Some people hold it like a pen, others hold it inside the palm pressed against the inside of the first two, or all four, fingers by the right hand thumb. Experiment to find your own most comfortable hold.

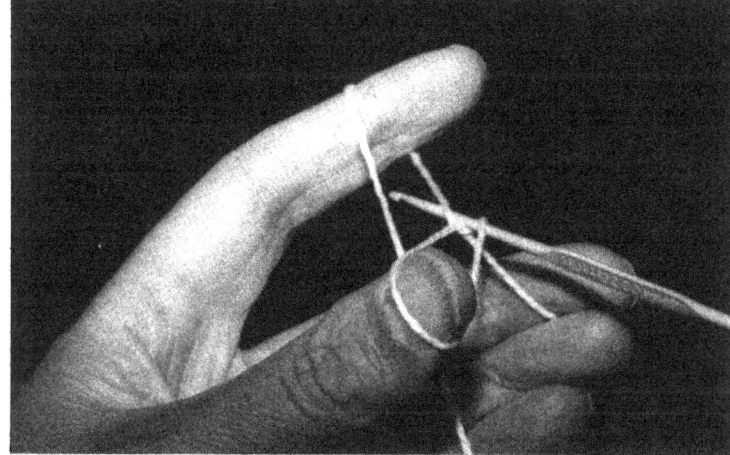

Making a Slip Knot and First Loop.

Threading the Yarn:

The yarn is **tensioned** by being threaded through the fingers of the **left** hand. **Thread** the yarn from the yarn ball kept at the back of the left hand, between the little finger and the third finger, up to and clockwise round the index finger, so bringing it round to the front. Hold the yarn tail or the fabric between the thumb and the middle finger.

Some people prefer to wind the yarn anticlockwise round the index finger, others hold the fabric between index finger and thumb and thread the yarn round the middle finger. Find your own preference. If you need extra tension for fine yarns, wind the yarn once round the little finger before bringing it through to thread over another finger.

Slip Knot:

Thread the yarn as explained above. Bring it forward from the index or middle finger, take it round the thumb clockwise from front to back, so forming a loop round the thumb. Hold the yarn end between the second and third fingers. Insert the hook under the loop, twist it under the thread (coming from the index finger) outside the loop and draw the yarn through the loop. Release the loop from the thumb and pull to tighten the knot; the slip knot and first loop will be ready on the needle.

BASIC CROCHET STITCHES

Chain Stitch (ABBREVIATION: ch):

Make a **slip knot** as explained above; a loop is on the crochet needle. Holding the yarn tail between thumb and desired finger, tighten the slip knot and draw the loop to make it slightly wider than the size of the crochet needle.

Yarn Round Hook (ABBREVIATION: yrh):

Twist the hook behind the yarn on the right hand side of the index finger (so that it comes clockwise from behind to the front of the hook). This action is called **yarn round hook** (ABBREVIATION: yrh). Now slip the loop on the barrel (the straight part) to the shank (the narrow part) of the crochet needle and draw through a loop. You have made one chain stitch. The size of the chain stitch is controlled by the size of the barrel of the crochet needle, analogous to knitted loops on a knitting needle.

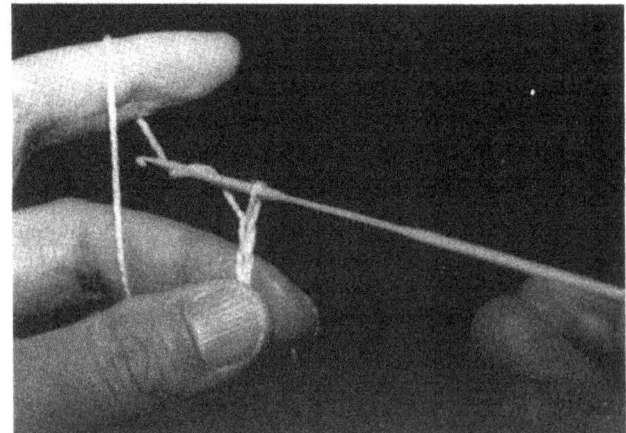

Yarn around hook (yrh) and making a Crochet Chain.

Foundation or Base Chain:

Continue to draw through the desired number of loops to make a simple crochet foundation chain.

Starting or Turning Chains:

All crochet stitches have height. In order to have an even finish, whether working in rows or in rounds, a certain number of chain stitches must be added at the beginning of each row or round to replace the first stitch and to prepare the work for the next row or round. Miss out the first stitch (or equivalent length of chain) after the needle to compensate for the replaced stitch. The number of starting or turning chains required depends on the height of the stitch to follow. In general, you will need no extra chain to start a slip stitch row or round, 1 extra chain to start double crochet rows or rounds, 2 ch for half trebles, 3 ch for trebles and so on. **Finish** rows or rounds by working into the top (last) turning or starting chain of the previous row or round. The turning chains and finish are often specified in Irish Crochet patterns, so simply follow the instructions. Work is also occasionally done in a **spiral**, in which case no turning or starting chains are needed.

IMPORTANT NOTE: All crochet stitches other than chains, and sometimes stitches worked over padding, are worked into the stitches of the previous row. The top of each stitch shows as a horizontal loop (a chain) with **two** sections - a front and a back horizontal yarn bar. Crocheting can be done in several ways, each with a different effect. The methods discussed here are simply the ones used in this book.

Basic Crochet:

Slip the hook under **both** horizontal bars of the stitch of the previous row. This method of making a stitch is always abbreviated in lower case letters in this book.

Ridged or Ribbed Crochet:

Slip the hook under only the **top** (back) horizontal bar of the stitch below. This method of making a stitch is abbreviated in upper case letters in this book.

Both methods are explained in detail under **Double Crochet** and the other basic crochet stitches are assumed to have been made in a similar way.

Slip Stitch (US Single Crochet) (ABBREVIATION: ss, SS):

Slip the hook, from the front to the back, under both the horizontal yarn bars of the next stitch on the left (2 loops on needle), yrh and draw through **both** loops to make a slip stitch.

Joining Stitch: Slip stitch is often used to join a foundation chain to form a ring, to connect one part of a design to another, or to take the yarn unobtrusively to another part of a fabric or motif without fastening off and starting again.

Basic Crochet Stitch.

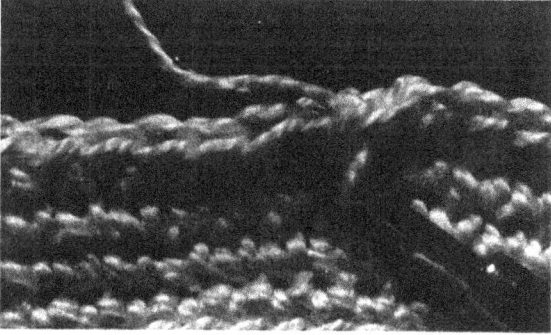
Ridge Crochet Stitch.

Double Crochet (US single crochet) (ABBREVIATION: dc, DC):

Slip the hook, from the front to the back, under **both** horizontal yarn bars of the next stitch to its left, yrh, draw through a loop (2 loops on needle). Yrh and draw a loop through **both** these loops; abbreviated dc.

A **ridged** (or ribbed) fabric is produced by slipping the hook under only the **top** (back) horizontal yarn bar of the previous row's stitch, yrh, draw through a loop (2 loops on needle), yrh, draw through a loop. This variation of double crochet, abbreviated DC, is a popular way of adding texture to many Irish Crochet motifs or parts of motifs.

Double Crochet Chain (ABBREVIATION: dcc):
Make a slip knot and work 1 ch. Make a dc into first chain.
*Double crochet into the yarn bar immediately to the left of the loop on the crochet needle and repeat from * until the chain is the required length. This makes a solid, rounded chain. (Illustrations on page 00.)
Alternatively, for a flat chain with a loopy edge, *double crochet into the **second** yarn bar immediately to the left of the loop on the needle and repeat from *.

Left to Right: Looped Double Crochet Chain. Rounded Double Crochet Chain. Crochet Chain.

Half Treble (US half double crochet) (ABBREVIATION: htr, HTR):
Put the yarn round the hook as if about to draw a loop through a stitch (yrh) and leave it there. Now slip the hook into the stitch on its left, yrh and draw through the yarn. There are now three loops on the needle. Yrh, draw a loop through all 3 loops to make a half treble.

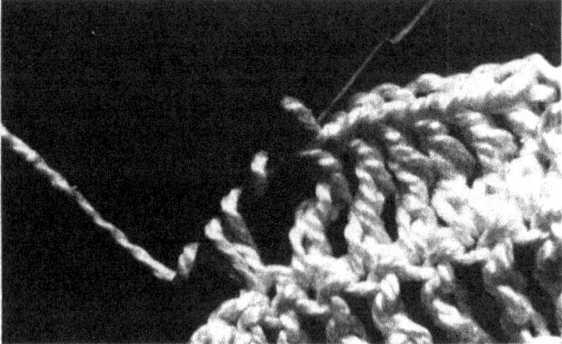

Half Treble (htr). Double Treble (dtr).

Treble (US double crochet) (ABBREVIATION: tr, TR):
Yrh. Now slip the hook into the stitch on its left and draw through a loop (3 loops on needle). Yrh, draw the yarn through the first 2 loops **only** (2 loops on needle). Yrh, draw the yarn through the remaining 2 loops to form a treble.

Double Treble (US treble) (ABBREVIATION: dtr, DTR):
Yrh twice (3 loops on needle). Slip the hook into the stitch on its left, yrh and draw through a loop (4 loops on needle). Yrh, draw the yarn through the first 2 loops (3 loops on needle). Yrh, draw the yarn through the next 2 loops (2 loops on needle). Yrh, draw the yarn through the last 2 loops to form a double treble.

Triple Treble (US double treble) (ABBREVIATION: tr tr, TR TR):
Yhr 3 times (4 loops on needle). Slip the hook into the stitch on its left, yrh and draw through a loop (5 loops on needle). Yrh, draw the yarn through the first 2 loops; continue to draw the yarn through 2 loops at a time until only 1 loop remains on the needle; the triple treble has been worked.

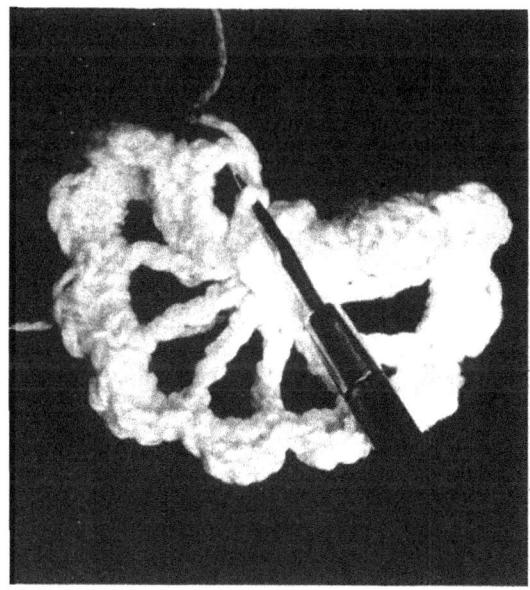
(a): Crocheting into the Back (dcb).

(b): Crocheting into the Back (dcb).

Crocheting into the Back (ABBREVIATION: dcb):
This technique is used to make overlapping crochet pieces, such as petals.
Instead of slipping the crochet hook under the horizontal yarn bars of the stitch of the previous row, **turn the back of the work to face you;** insert the hook under the **vertical** yarn bars, yrh and draw through a loop to form the first part of the stitch.
You will end up with a stitch finishing at the back of the work. See the **Rose Motif** instructions on page 15 for working the separate layers.
There are two ways of working into the back:
(a) Fold the fabric over, rotate it sideways and work the dcb.
(b) Turn the whole motif back to front, rotate it sideways and work the dcb. Work the whole round from the back, then turn the motif to the RHS to work the next round.

CROCHET ORNAMENTS

Chain Picot (ABBREVIATION: P):
Picots are used to decorate motif outlines, or to make chain picot bar fillings.

Make a crochet stitch. Now make 1, 2, 3 or more chains, slip stitch or double crochet into the first of these chains. This forms a 1, 2, 3 or more chain picot.

Picot Chain: *Work 1, 2, 3 or more chains, make a chain picot and repeat from * to form a foundation chain with regularly spaced chain picots.

Picot Border: *Work 1, 2 or 3 stitches in pattern. Make an appropriate chain picot and repeat from *. This makes a picot border **above** a row of crochet, and can be added on any outside curve to give a lighter, lacier look to the fabric.

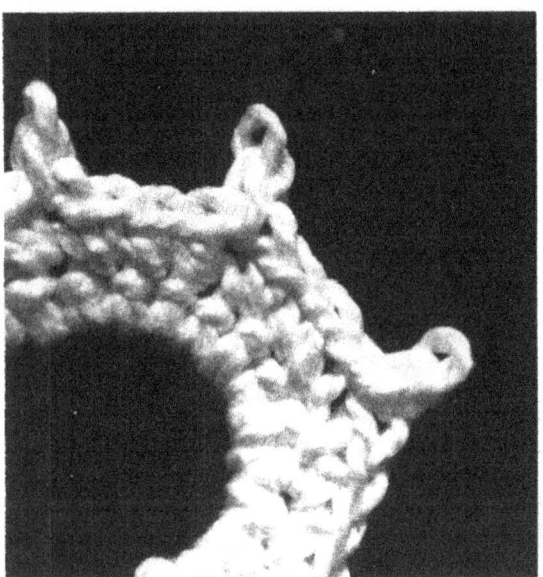

Picot Border.

Picot Chain.

Left to Right Chain Picot (ABBREVIATION: Pb):
These picots are useful when working chain picot bars from left to right; the picots will then point upwards, like the chain picots worked from right to left.

Make a crochet stitch. Now make 1, 2, 3 or more chains, elongate the last chain, take the hook out, slip it through the first chain made and through the elongated chain, yrh and draw through to make a **L to R Picot**.

Left to Right Picot Chain: * Work 1, 2, 3 or more chains, make an appropriate L to R picot and repeat from *.

The Clones Knot:
These special knots are used to decorate motifs, or to make specially ornate fillings. To make them easily and uniformly takes practice.

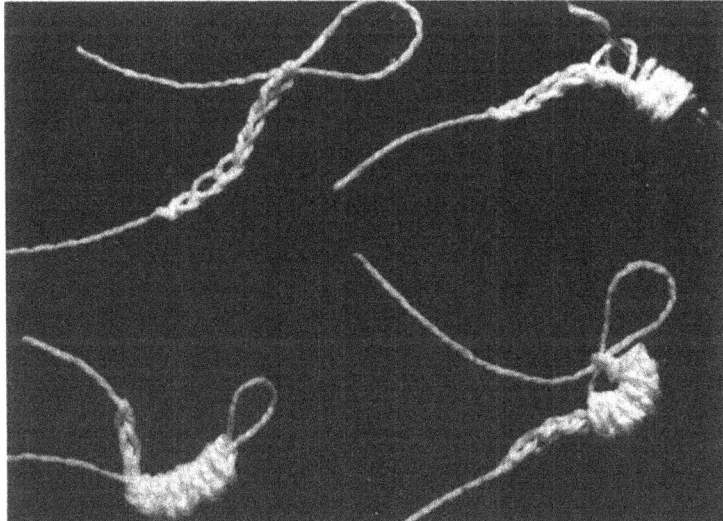

Four stages of a Clones Knot.

Round Knot:
Work 5, 6 or 7 ch. **Elongate the last chain slightly so that it slips **very easily** over the barrel of the crochet needle.

*Yrh, put the hook **under** the chain, yrh (clockwise, as first yrh) and pull hook above chain, elongating yarn so that the crochet needle lies parallel to the top of the chain. Repeat from * at least 5 times (so that there are 10 yrhs on the needle), more for a fuller knot. Yrh, draw through **all loops on needle,** push loops together if necessary and ss to 4th, 5th or 6th ch.

Long Knot:
Work 5, 6 or 7 ch. **Elongate the last chain slightly so that it slips **very easily** over the barrel of the crochet needle.

*Yrh, put the hook **under** the chain, yrh (clockwise, as first yrh), elongating yarn so that the crochet needle lies parallel to the top of the chain. Repeat from * at least 5 times (so that there are 10 yrhs on the needle), more for a fuller knot. Make a dc in 3rd ch from needle, yrh and draw through all loops on needle, make a dc into same ch as before.

Repeat from ** for either knot to make a **Clones Knot Chain.**

The secret of making a successful **Clones Knot** is to use a high quality, smooth crochet needle with a hook no wider than the barrel. Make sure the yrh loops are **deep enough and** that the yarn is **always** put round the hook from back to front (clockwise). If your knot is too loose for your liking, use a finer crochet needle for making the knot than for the rest of the work. With practice you will find it quite quick and easy to make good, even knots. Some of the old workers had 40 or more loops in a single knot!

CROCHETING WITH PADDING

Crocheting over padding of any sort is very simply carried out. Double crochet over padding is described in detail below: anchor the padding cord between the first loops when crocheting off for a treble or an even higher stitch.

Crocheting over Foundation Chains: Crochet chains (often joined into a ring) are also used as padding; simply treat the foundation chain as a padding cord, and follow the directions below.

Double Crochet over Padding: Start with a loop on the needle, put the hook **under** the padding cord, yrh and pull hook up above padding cord (2 loops on needle). Yrh, draw a loop through both loops on needle. Make as many stitches as are needed to cover the padding - push them together to make a good, tight covering.

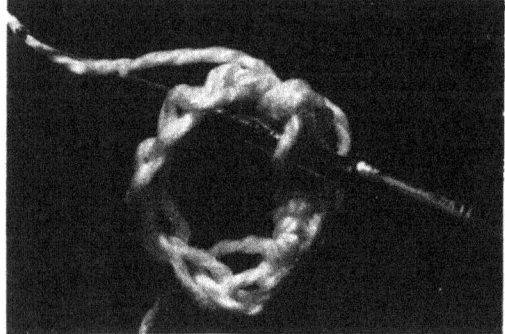

Double Crochet over Chain Ring.　　　　　　　　　　　　UCA, Double Crochet over padding folded in half.

Bosses: These rings are padded by winding the crocheting or padding yarn many times round a mesh gauge. If this seems difficult at first try using very small curtain rings instead of padding, using several on top of each other if necessary. Make sure they are rustproof!

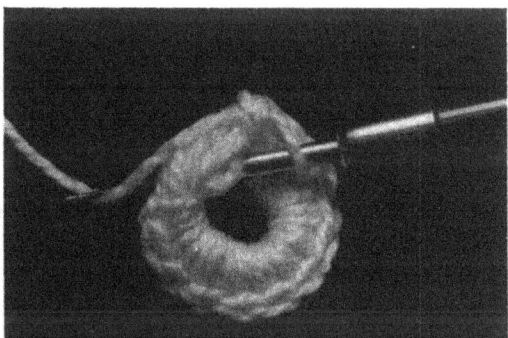

Padding cord wound over mesh gauge and barrel of crochet needle.　　　　　　　　Finishing a Boss.

Use Cord Alone (ABBREVIATION: UCA):
The abbreviation UCA is used when the stitches are worked over padding **only**.

Ring Start: Make a loop with padding cord and follow the directions for working double crochet over padding, the normal method of covering the padding.

You will see that, in order to form a small circle, the ends of the padding yarn can be pulled to the desired size - this can be done after several rows or rounds of the motif have been worked, as this makes it easier to work the first part of the motif.

Straight Start: Allow sufficient padding cord for the piece to be worked (given in the instructions). Crochet **across** the central fold to anchor the start of the padding cord; it can then be tightened to any desired shape without fear of pulling it out.

Boss Start: Use a large-size knitting needle as a convenient mesh gauge. Make a slip knot and first loop with the crocheting yarn and hook, lay the barrel along the knitting needle and wind the yarn round **both** for the number of times stated in the pattern.

Yrh, draw a loop through centre of ring while pulling the wound yarn off the top of the knitting needle. Hold yarn loops between finger and thumb of left hand. *Yrh, draw yarn through the 2 loops on the crochet needle, yrh, draw through centre of ring and repeat from * until the ring is completely filled with dcs. Patterns generally give a number to crochet, but once you are used to this method of crocheting you will not need to count.

Use Cord (ABBREVIATION: UC):
Generally speaking, padding is used for relief at the central and outside edges of many motifs. The abbreviation UC precedes sections where the crocheting is to be done over padding **and** into a previously crocheted row or round.

Leave Cord (ABBREVIATION: LC):
It is often helpful to leave a length of padding yarn hanging at a specific part of the design, rather than cutting it, to be picked up later when it may again be useful.

Tighten Cord (ABBREVIATION: TC):
Please **NOTE CAREFULLY** that each **individual** padding strand should be tightened separately to ensure an even tension.

If two adjoining padded sections are to be curved, tension the inside curve more than the outside curve so that the complete piece lies in a smooth curve.

Turning When Using Padding Cord:
Padded sections can be turned, or twisted back on themselves, by working over the padding cord **only** for a feew stitches. Resume ordinary work after the turn.

JOINS

Joining into Rings:
A slip stitch is generally used to join the last to the first stitch of a foundation chain to form a round or ring.

Joining Rounds:
Rounds are also joined with slip stitches. In order to finish with the correct height, the slip stitch is worked into the last made of the starting or turning chains.

Joining chains into a ring.

Double Crochet Join (dcj).

Joining Motifs:
Motifs are often joined - to form sprigs, for example.

Left Join: To join to a motif or fabric to the **left** of the work in progress, crochet the last one or two stitches into the place you want to join to, using the stitches of the motif or fabric as foundation stitches.

Flat or Right Join: To join to a motif or fabric to the **right** of the work in progress, **enlarge** the last loop on the needle, slip the hook out, insert it into the place you wish to join to, replace the loop on the hook, draw it through and pull it to the proper size, then complete the crochet stitch. This will make a **flat** join.

It is sometimes easier to **sew** crocheted pieces together rather than to crochet them together.

Double Crochet Join (ABBREVIATION: dcj):
To join previously made chain loops, insert the hook under the first chain loop, yrh, draw through a loop; insert the hook under the second chain loop, yrh, draw through a loop; yrh, draw through all three loops on the needle.

Joining Padding:
If you need to join in extra padding, overlap one fold at a time so that you avoid an unsightly bulge at the join.

MISCELLANEOUS TECHNIQUES

Simple Increase:
Simple increases are made by working 2 dc (2 DC), or any other two stitches, into the same stitch.

Avoid Cutting Yarn:
A good way to avoid cutting the crocheting yarn is to slip stitch along certain parts of the motif being made to reach a part you wish to restart from.

If you intend to use padding yarn for an outside curve, plan ahead to leave some padding yarn hanging at an appropriate point. Then simply draw the crochet yarn package through an enlarged last loop to fasten off, lay it along the top of the row to be used as a foundation for working over padding, lay the padding yarn along that also and crochet over **both**; this is a particularly useful way to finish many designs.

Shaping Rings & Coils:
Small rings and bosses are automatically shaped by the thick layers of yarn relative to their size; larger rings and coils need to be shaped to look well.

Coils only look well if they are all the same shape; this is most readily achieved by passing a very thick knitting needle, or some other mesh gauge, through the openings and **pinching** the coils into shape - secure them in that shape to hold them in place for filling. Large rings will also need shaping; pinch the material between forefinger and thumb until you get the desired shape.

FASTENING OFF

An important part of finishing the many motifs is to fasten both the crocheting yarn and the padding yarn off securely and neatly.

Traditional Method: Cut a 20 cm (8 ins) length of the crocheting yarn, draw it through the last loop on the needle, and pull tight. This fastens the yarn off securely.

Thread the yarn through an appropriate tapestry needle, tighten any padding to the desired length, then sew the padding securely to the underside of the motif. Darn in the yarn end and cut off.

Modern Method: Cut the crocheting yarn and draw through the last loop, as above. Tighten any padding, attach it to the back of the motif with a fabric adhesive, attach the crocheting yarn and leave to dry. Tap the sections together by wrapping a piece of cling film round the end of a pencil, crochet needle or your index finger. Cut off excess yarn when the pieces are glued together. No sewing!

Alternatively, **bond** the yarns to the crocheting using a fabric bond.

You can, of course, use this method to attach your motifs to the lace ground, or to attach parts of a lace ground to the motifs, but this may make the lace too stiff.

It is useful to leave all the neatening and bonding or glueing until you are ready to add the filling.

LACEMAKING METHODS CONTENTS

	Page
Order of Working	81
Arranging the Design	82
The Materials	
Crochet Hooks or Needles	83
Round Meshes	83
Sewing Needles	84
Yarns	84
Yarn Gauge	84
Padding Cord	84
Pattern Foundation	85
Attaching the Sprigs	85
Filling	86
Connecting Motifs to Mesh	
Applied onto Background	86
Set into Medallions	86
Connected by Filling	87
Filling Methods	88
Practising Fillings	89
Open Space Filling	89
Solid Picot Filling	90
Clones Knot Filling	91
Single Picot Bar Filling	92
Double Picot Bar Filling	92
Banding the Lace Outline	
Banding Row	93
Multi-picot Edging	93
Crown Edging	94
Daisy Edging	94
Rosette Edging	95
Three-Loop Edging	95
Six-Loop Edging	95

LACEMAKING METHODS

ORDER OF WORKING

Follow the eight steps below to work a piece of Irish Crochet Lace. Each step is explained in detail to help beginners to the craft.

(1) Arranging the design.
(2) Choosing and collecting the materials.
(3) Preparing the pattern foundation.
(4) Working the sprigs, and a chain or picot chain outline if used.
(5) Securing the sprigs and any outline to the pattern foundation.
(6) Filling.
(7) Banding (if no outline has been used).
(8) Edging.

Copier cut-outs placed to form a new design.

ARRANGING THE DESIGN

Choose one of the designs from this book. Alternatively, simply choose a shape you wish to work in Irish Crochet Lace, together with motifs or complete sprigs which you would like to use for this shape.

An exciting, and certainly a most creative, aspect of working Irish Crochet Lace is to assemble the sprigs into a pleasing design. Specific pattern instructions are given in this book, but do remember that you can develop your own designs from any of the given motifs.

If you are following one of the patterns simply arrange the design on a suitable foundation, as explained below. If, however, you would like to adjust the design in some way, or to use the motifs arranged into a different shape, you may find my technique useful:

Crochet one example of each of the motifs you wish to use, using white crochet yarn of the thickness you intend to use, together with the hook you will use for the whole project. You need not make the stems, white knitting ribbon can be cut to size and curved as necessary. Take the completed motifs to the nearest copier, lay them **face down** and cover them with black card. Take as many copies as you need, preferably onto white card.

Cut out your motifs, which will show the detail quite well. Now cut a piece of black backing (or self-adhesive vinyl backing, see (b) under PATTERN FOUNDATION) to the shape you wish to make. Lay the motifs on this shape, arranging them until you have a design you like. Take your time, juggle them about. It is useful to have a few extra small motifs just in case you wish to fill awkward spaces. Arrange, and curve, appropriate lengths of knitting ribbon to represent the stems and to display them in pleasing curves. Alternatively, you could use a white pencil to sketch in the stems. Arrange more ribbon to represent an outline if you intend to crochet one.

When you are satisfied with the design attach the pieces to the backing by pinning, sewing or glueing them on. Take a copy of the design; this will be your pattern base.

Transparency Material: The easiest and quickest way to mount your design on a pattern foundation is to copy the design onto transparent material. You need to be able to work on the reverse side because the copied design might stain your lace. Symmetrical patterns can simply be used **upside down;** asymmetric patterns need to be copied again, this time from the **reversed** transparent material.

Large designs can be copied in sections. The complete design can now be mounted onto a suitable pattern foundation as explained under that heading.

THE MATERIALS

It is useful to keep all the materials together in a **container**.
Small plastic bags are useful for keeping each type of motif separate and clean.
You will need **scissors** to cut padding and working yarns.

Crochet Hooks or Needles:
Fine, steel crochet hooks are available in the following sizes:

Metric (mm)	British	US
.60	6	14 - 13
.75	5	12 - 11
1.00	4	10 - 9
1.25	3	8 - 7
1.50	2.5	6 - 5
1.75	2	4 - 3

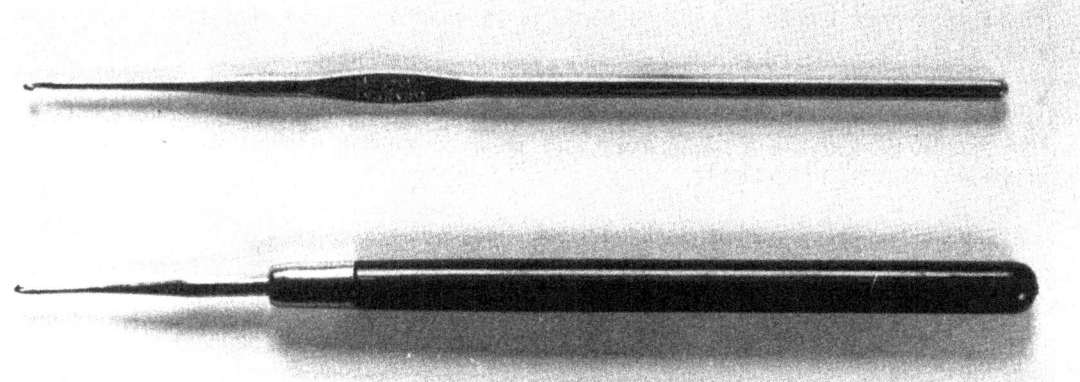

Steel crochet hooks, with and without a plastic handle.

Always use the finest hook you can manage, since Irish Crochet Lace needs to be worked as tightly as possible for the best results. You may prefer to start with the 1.00 mm size to give yourself a chance to get used to working with a fine hook.

Traditionally, the recommended steel hooks had cork handles. This avoids finger cramp and the hook getting too hot when in use. The nearest modern equivalents are steel hooks with plastic handles. (See Inside Back Cover.)

The smaller sizes of the excellent anodised aluminium hooks can be used for wools and yarns of **Silver Gauge** category medium fine and heavier.

Round meshes: Gauges for making ring foundations are readily available in the form of large-size knitting needles, small bottle corks or even finger tips!

Sewing needles: Use tapestry needles with an adequately large eye and blunt ends to avoid splitting the crochet yarn when sewing.

Yarns: The traditional Irish Crochet Lace designs in this book were worked in Coats Mercer Crochet cotton as this is readily available and of high quality. However, any fine crocheting yarn can be used as a substitute; many of these are offered in several solid colours as well as in ombré shades. Furthermore, sewing and embroidery threads, fine silks, synthetic threads, tinsels and fine linens are all suitable. Do bear in mind that it is **very important** to use only the highest quality yarns so that your laces last for as long as possible. **Always** test a new yarn by working samples of both motifs and lace ground to see if you like the result and to test the tension and the reaction to washing.

Thicker yarns, including wool, can also be used to make some of the motifs and edgings. Though not Irish Crochet **Lace,** such pieces make wonderful ornaments and trimmings for plain knitted or crocheted garments or other articles.

Yarn Gauge: The Lorant yarn gauge - the **Silver Gauge** - has been used to categorise yarn sizes so that appropriate substitute yarns can be used for the patterns in this book.

Padding Cord: Padding yarn or cord foundations can be made by using several strands of the crocheting yarn, or fewer strands of a thicker version of the crocheting yarn. It can be difficult to manage several strands at first; thick, smooth knitting cottons or linens make a good substitute. Be careful to match the colour of the padding to the colour of the crocheting yarn and wash a sample padded piece to check the relative shrinkage of the yarns.

Pattern Foundation: Professional Irish Crochet workers simply use stout brown paper for their pattern foundation. This can be used, but tends to be difficult to handle for a beginner. Modern alternatives are suggested here.

A yarn gauge: The Silver Gauge.

PATTERN FOUNDATION

The ease with which a beginner can successfully connect Irish Lace motifs by 'filling' the spaces between them with a crochet mesh or lace ground, once that technique has been mastered, depends largely on the pattern foundation. Most modern books recommend a fabric backing for a stout brown paper base.

I have a few suggestions which make use of modern materials:

(a) Iron a strong adhesive interlining onto a stout paper (or your copied design) to make a sturdy base with a non-slip backing.

(b) Use a self-adhesive vinyl in a contrasting colour to the yarn you are using. I favour green 'Fablon' because this is a restful colour for light laces, and because the backing doesn't slip too much. This material is very tough, and once you are experienced you need not even bother to **sew** the motifs into place. Simply cut out, and peel off, the backing paper on the space to be occupied by the motif and **stick** this on. When all the motifs are in place you can connect them with fillings worked over the remaining backing paper. When the lace is complete, simply **peel** it off its backing. Pin the drawn or copied design over the backing paper before you start.

You may even like to adapt this method for joining medallions. Leave a strip of backing paper between two wide strips of adhesive vinyl. Stick the medallions to be joined on either side of the paper strip; this will hold them securely in place while you work the join.

(c) Buy a suitably patterned curtain lace and secure the motifs to this; strengthen the back with adhesive interlining or a suitable substitute. The spaces for filling are now shown in a grid which you can use as a pattern guide for the filling.

ATTACHING THE SPRIGS TO THE FOUNDATION

Traditionally, the sprigs were securely hand sewn in place on the foundation according to the design pattern. Stems were carefully curved and secured in that curve.

Modern lacemakers are not always good hand sewers but it is relatively easy to oversew the outlines and the stems. Use contrasting thread so that you can remove it more readily when the lace is finished. Alternatively, use the zig zag stitch on your sewing machine to attach reasonably flat sprigs to the pattern foundation. Thread the machine with contrast thread, and make a trial piece.

Use **invisible nylon** to permanently sew stems to motifs, or for any other permanent sewing you would prefer to be invisible. Inexpert stitches will not show up.

Consider using self-adhesive vinyl for a pattern foundation. You may still have to oversew the outlines of the motifs, but even that is easier to accomplish when the centre is already attached.

FILLING

The **filling** is the background crochet net or mesh - the lace ground - connecting the motifs. There are three ways of connecting the motifs and the filling, and several types of crochet mesh which make appropriate fillings. Several filling patterns are given below; these can be used interchangeably for connecting any set of motifs.

Fillings were traditionally worked in the same yarn as the motifs. However, Eithne d'Arcy, in her **Irish Crochet Lace** (Dolmen, 1984) recommends working the filling in a heavier grade of the same make of crochet yarn used for the motifs. This helps to balance the weight of the more elaborate sprigs.

A good deal of 'filling' difficulty can be overcome by fitting your motifs closely together. When you are left with largish spaces, consider whether to add further small motifs and whether to adjust the design accordingly. If you prefer well-spaced sprigs, I suggest you might consider using a heavier type of filling, such as the **Solid Picot Filling** detailed below. Alternatively, you could replace the single chains used in the lighter fillings by double crochet chains.

CONNECTING MOTIFS AND BACKGROUND MESH

There are three methods of connecting the motifs and the filling:

(1) Motifs Applied onto Mesh Background:
The simplest method of all is to work a piece of crochet mesh, shaping it to the pattern foundation you wish to use. When this basic lace ground is complete, simply attach motifs onto it at appropriate points. You may like to consider using some of the bonding tapes or powders to fuse your pieces to the mesh background. You might prefer to secure the outlines by sewing them on from the **back;** using invisible nylon as a sewing thread will minimize problems about stitches showing on the right side.

The lace ground can also be a bought, machined netting. This makes an attractive lace, and this type of lace ground may be more delicate than a crocheted one.

(2) Motifs Set into Medallions:
Small motifs, such as the relatively simple **Rose** or **Shamrock** motifs used for the **Christening Apron** (pages 52 and 55), are often made into medallions by surrounding them with single or double picot bars as soon as the motif has been worked. The square is the preferred medallion shape, but triangles are also used. Small 'crown' shapes radiating out from the motif add interest. The completed medallions are then 'invisibly' joined with single or double picot bars. This type of work is often called **Baby Irish Crochet Lace,** since the motifs are smaller and more delicate than many Irish Lace Motifs.

Joining Medallions:
For the neatest effect, **flat join** from left to right and use a **L to R** chain picot.

Single Picot Bars: Work 1 dc into a suitable corner of a medallion square, *1 chain picot (size as filling in medallions), 1 ch, 1 dc into an appropriate place on the medallion to be joined, 2 ch, 1 dc into the next appropriate place on the first medallion. Repeat from *. The join will be quite invisible.

Double Picot Bars: Work 1 dc into a suitable corner of a medallion square, *1 chain picot (size as filling), 1 ch, 1 dc into appropriate place on medallion to be joined, 1 chain picot, 2 ch, 1 dc into next appropriate place on first medallion. Repeat from *.

(3) **Motifs Connected by Filling:**

Here the complete 'spread' of the different sprigs to be used for a pattern is securely attached to a pattern foundation shape. This may also have a crocheted outline. The filling is worked by crocheting a chosen mesh bar pattern between the secured sprigs. No specific instructions can be given in the patterns since each crocheter will need to judge how best to connect the motifs when actually working the background. It is useful to practise the filling you intend to use.

Special Points:

There are some important points to bear in mind when working this type of filling:

(a) It is **essential** to make a mesh which will lie flat - not too tight and not too loose. Otherwise the whole design will pucker when it is taken from the pattern foundation.

(b) In order to work easily, and to see what you are doing, **fold** the foundation back along the line of work. Flatten the foundation out again to make sure you have worked to the correct tension before going on to the next row.

(c) It may be easier to work outwards from a corner than in straight rows, as explained in the instructions for the **Solid Picot Filling.**

(d) Remember that the filling **pattern** gives you a fixed length for your bar (bride). Try to keep to this length as it will make your filling as even as possible, but do remember that you can alter it at any stage to accommodate your filling to the shape you wish to fill - simply use fewer, or more, chains to achieve your bar and leave out any picots or knots where necessary.

Using Reversible Fillings:

Most fillings are reversible. This gives you the opportunity to arrange your designs **face down** on your pattern foundation and to work the filling over the **back** of the design. The advantage is that you can slip stitch across, or chain over, narrow stems to make the filling easier to carry out and to avoid fastening off too frequently.

Sew (or stick) your main motifs to the pattern foundation. Then add the stems, curving them pleasingly and overlapping onto the flowers and leaves so that they appear natural. Sew the stems securely in place before starting the filling.

Non-reversible Fillings:

Non-reversible fillings will need to be added to the **front** of the design for the best effect. Sew (or stick) your motifs onto the pattern foundation, then add the stems so that they lie **under** the main motifs. Sew (or stick) all the pieces in place before filling.

FILLING METHODS

Perhaps the most difficult part of making successful Irish Crochet Lace for a beginner is to execute the fillings correctly. This is something which has to be practised. As each crocheter will have her own tension, the **number** and/or **length** of the filling bars (brides) needed for the lace to lie correctly will depend on individual tension, and the crocheter will have to use her judgment and experience to carry the filling out successfully.

Start each type of filling, at any convenient point in the pattern, by working 1 dc into a convenient place on an edge or corner of a motif, or into the chain, or picot chain, outline. Note that each filling is given as a bar pattern which will form an arc. **Halve** the bar length to find the points of attachment along the outlines of the space to be filled (see the **Open Space Filling**).

Most fillings can be continuously worked from right to left by turning the foundation between each row; this method can be easier for a beginner to manage than working alternate rows from left to right, using the **flat join.**

The biggest stumbling block for many newcomers to Irish Crochet Lace is to decide on **where to go next** when working a filling; only practice will show you how to continue, and each worker will need to find her own methods. Once you have the

Avoid fastening off, since this involves bonding or darning in ends. Left and right hand side edges may have to be created by working short lengths of chain to form the relevant selvedge.

The important point is to make the lace spaces **as uniform as possible,** and to keep the mesh **at the correct tension.** Do try not to give up Irish Crochet Lace because of initial difficulties with the fillings; try to concentrate on a simple one which you have no trouble in making, then go on to more adventurous fillings as you gain confidence.

Bought laces used to form spaces for filling practice.

PRACTISING FILLINGS

Buy an inexpensive narrow lace. Sew or bond different shapes outlined by this lace securely to a pattern foundation. This will give you practice spaces to fill without the labour of making motifs or a crochet outline.

Open Space Filling:

This is, perhaps, the simplest of all the fillings and can readily be made even by a beginner.

Row 1: Work 1 dc into a convenient place, *6 ch (or whatever number you find suitable), **halve** this length and note the next place to attach the filling, 1 dc into this place: repeat from * until you reach the left hand side of the space to be filled.

Row 2 and following rows: Turn the work, or work from left to right, as you prefer. Attach the last ch with a double crochet further up the left hand side of the space to be filled (attaching it to a motif or foundation outline), turn and work the same size bars, attaching each one with a double crochet over the arcs of the previous row. Finish by attaching the last chain to the right hand side, working the appropriate number of chain and finishing higher up on this side.

This is a very easy filling and the number of chains made can be varied as needed. It is a simple, dainty filling and has the added advantage of being reversible.

Use a double crochet chain for a heavier filling, or work a return row of dc over the arcs as explained in the next example.

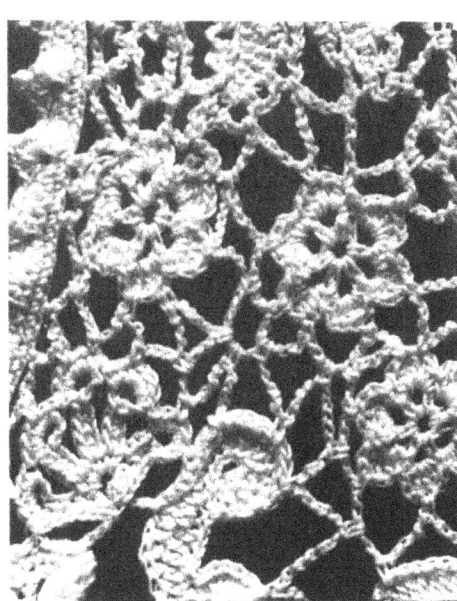

Detail of Open Space Filling

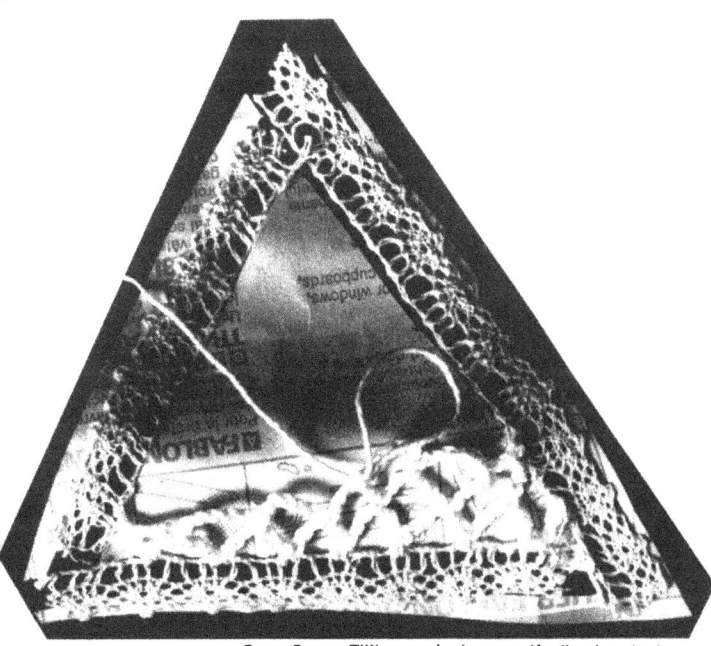

Open Space Filling worked over self-adhesive vinyl. Note fold-back for easier working.

Solid Picot Filling:
This particular example of working filling is shown worked from the left hand corner outwards - it shows in detail how the irregular spaces between motifs can be filled with a two-row filling pattern.

Arrange a rectangular crochet outline by making 70 ch and joining with 1 ss. Now work 15 tr, 3 ch for a corner, 20 tr, 3 ch, 15 tr, 3 ch, 20 tr, 3 ch and ss to join. Fasten off. Attach this crochet rectangle outline firmly to a good foundation, placing it **right** side down to show up the edge loops distinctly.

PL = 6 chain picot loop.

Ss into left hand corner and work 1 PL. Ss into the 5th st from the bottom on the left hand selvedge. Work 7 ch; join to next point as follows: take the hook out of the last loop, slip the hook through the 4th st from the LHS on the bottom selvedge, slip the open loop over the hook again and pull through a loop.

You now have a simple chain connecting two points. Fold back the foundation and work over this chain, from right to left, as follows: work 4 dc over the 7 ch lp up to the centre of the loop; make 1 PL, work 4 more dc over the rest of the 7 ch loop. The first solid bar, together with its picot, is now complete. You are back at the LH selvedge.

Ss up the LH selvedge with 4 ss; make 4 ch, join (as above) to the 3rd dc from LHS on 1st bar made, work 2 dc over the 4 ch loop, made 8 ch, join (as above) to 2nd dc on RHS of picot of bar made, work 4 dc on 8 ch loop, make 2 ch, join to the 7th st from RHS on bottom selvedge, make 3 dc on the 2 ch lp, work 4 dc, 1 PL, 4 dc on the 8 ch lp, 3 dc on the remaining 3 ch lp, ss to LHS selvedge.

Work 7 ch, join to 2nd dc on LHS of last picot made, work 2 dc over the 7 ch lp, make 8 ch, join to 3rd st on RHS of last PL, 3 dc over the 8 ch lp, 7 ch, join to the centre of the 3 dc below, 2 dc over the 7 ch lp, 3 ch, join to the bottom selvedge 3 sts to the RHS of last join.

Work 3 dc, 1 PL, 3 dc on the 3 ch lp, work 3 dc over the last 7 ch lp, make 6 ch, join to bottom selvedge 3 sts along to the right of last join, make 4 dc on 6 ch lp, join to RHS selvedge 5 sts up from bottom, make 3 dc, 1 PL, 3 dc on the 6 ch lp, 1 dc on remainder of next lp, 3 dc, 1 PL, 3 dc on 7 ch lp, 3 dc, 1 PL, 3 dc on next ch lp, 1 ss into LHS selvedge.

Work 4 ss up the LHS selvedge; 4 ch, join to left of last PL, 3 dc on 4 ch lp, 6 ch, join to left of next PL, 3 dc on 6 ch bar; 8 ch, join to right of same PL, 3 dc over the 8 ch lp.

The working of this filling should, by now, be clear and it should be possible for you to finish the space without further specific instructions.

Please note that the chain bars **must** all go from left to right, since the working over the chain bars goes from right to left. The **numbers** of chains worked are for an average tension - if yours varies from the normal, work more or fewer chains, or change to a different hook size.

The illustration has been worked in relatively heavy yarn to show the individual stitches clearly.

MORE FILLING PATTERNS

Reversible Clones Knot Filling:
Row 1: Join to a convenient place with 1 dc. 7 ch, *make a **Long Clones Knot** (page 76), 7 ch. Miss sufficient space along an edge, then join with 1 dc. Repeat from * to the end of the row.

Row 2 and following rows: Work as Row 1, but working 1 dc into the arc **after** the knot in the previous row.

Non-reversible Clones Knot Filling:
Row 1: Join to a convenient place with 1 dc. *6 ch, make a **Clones Knot** (page 76), 6 ch. Miss sufficient space along an edge, then join with 1 dc. Repeat from * to the end of the row.

Row 2 and following even rows: Working from L to R; *6 ch, make a knot, 6 ch, elongate the loop on the hook, take it out, slip it under the arc before the next knot of the previous row, draw through the loop, yrh, draw through a loop, put the yarn **behind** the knot, put the hook under the arc after the knot, yrh, draw through a loop (2 loops on hook), yrh, draw through both loops. Repeat from * to the end of the row.

Following odd rows: *6 ch, make a knot, 6 ch, 1 dc **before** knot on last row, keep yarn at the back of the knot, 1 dc **after** knot on last row, repeat from *.

The knots will all lean to the **back** of the fabric so that you can join the back of the motifs (see page 87). If you prefer the knot on the front, always bring the yarn to the **front** of the knot of the previous row before working the connecting stitches on either side of the knot.

Solid Picot Filling.

Detail of Clones Knot Filling.

Single Picot Bar Filling:

Row 1: Join to a convenient place with 1 dc. *7 ch, 1 dc in 5th ch from hook, 2 ch, 1 dc, miss sufficient space along an edge, then join with 1 dc. Repeat from * to the end of the row.

Row 2: Work as Row 1, but working 1 dc **after** the picot over the arcs of the previous row.

This is a slightly more ornamental lace ground, easy to work and also reversible. The bars can be made longer or shorter, as necessary, by adding or leaving out some of the chains.

You can alter the size of the picot, the length of the chains between picots and even substitute double crochet chain for ordinary chain.

Double Picot Bar Filling:

Row 1: Join to a convenient place with 1 dc. *7 ch, 1 dc into 5th ch from hook, 7 ch, 1 dc into 5th ch from hook, 2 ch, miss sufficient space along an edge, then join with 1 dc. Repeat from * until the end of the row.

Row 2 and following rows: Work as Row 1, but working 1 dc between the picots of the arcs of the previous row.

Though it looks a little more ornate than the previous fillings, it is no more difficult than the **Single Picot Bar** and it is also reversible.

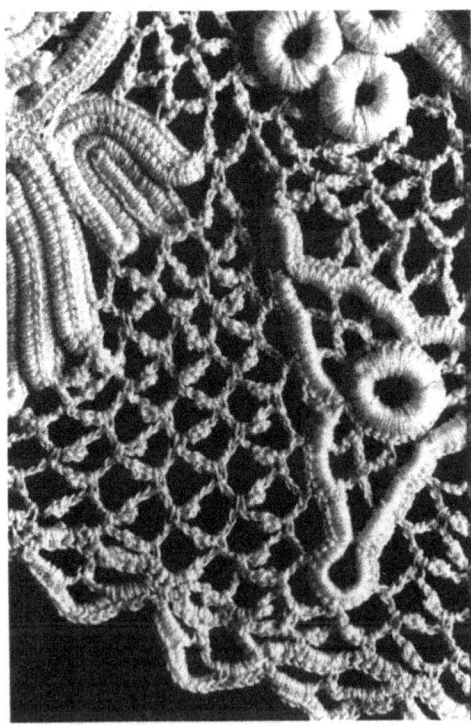

Detail of Single Picot Bar Filling.

Detail of Double Picot Bar Filling.

BANDING THE LACE OUTLINE

Some Irish Crochet Laces are edged by motif outlines, and no banding or edging apart from this is necessary. However, most Irish Crochet Laces are finished with a chain outline which is then edged with a suitable lace.

The simplest way to make the chain outline is simply to make a chain, or picot chain, of sufficient length to outline the pattern foundation, and to attach the outline to the foundation. Then work a banding row as explained below.

Alternatively, when the filling for an Irish Crochet Lace is being worked, approximate it as nearly as possible to the outline shape. Then finish the lace with a banding or trimming row which will even up any irregularities. This row is always worked on the same principle, though the actual stitch sequence will depend on the particular circumstances.

Banding Row:
Attach the yarn to a suitable place at the end of the filling. The band is made, for example, by working 5 ch, *1 dc, 3 ch, miss out space of 3 ch and repeat from * until the outline is complete. Ss to 2nd ch made.

Precise instructions are not possible, since it may be necessary to lengthen the double crochet to a triple, a double triple or even a triple triple to make an even outline. The band should finish with an even line of chain, above a regular set of chain spaces, outlining the lace.

Use whatever chain space (such as 2, 3, 4 or even more) you may prefer, or whatever interval length suits the edging you intend to add. The basic stitch used between the chain spaces is often a triple rather than a double crochet. The lace can be removed from the pattern foundation after the banding is complete. Simply cut the contrast threads securing the lace to the foundation and remove the thread ends.

Edgings:
There are several types of traditional edging patterns, and some are given in the pattern directions. A few more are included below so that you can vary the edging if you like. Arrange the edging pattern symmetrically around the outline.

The edgings are normally worked on the right side only. Consequently, the direction of work changes quite frequently. The chain picots are abbreviated to P; the relevant picot size is given in each pattern. Please refer to the techniques section for working **flat joins** and **chain picots**.

Multi-picot Edging: (Multiple of three 4 ch spaces on a {1 tr, 4 ch, miss 4 sts} band).
P = 7 ch picot.
*R to L: 6 dc into 1st 4 ch sp, (3 dc, 1 P, 3 dc) into next 4 ch sp, 3 dc into next 4 ch sp;
L to R: 13 ch and flat join to middle of 1st 4 ch sp;
R to L: 2 dc, (5ch, 3 dc)7, 5 ch, 2 dc over 13 ch; finish with 3 dc into 3rd 4 ch sp.
Repeat from * along the whole outline.

Crown Edging: (Multiple of four 3 ch spaces on a {1 dc, 3 ch, miss 3 sts} band.)
P = 7 ch picot.
*R to L: (4 dc over next 3 ch)2, 3 dc over next 3 ch;
L to R: 10 ch, flat join to centre of 1st ch sp;
R to L: 17 dc over the 10 ch, 1 dc next to the 3 dc already made;
L to R: 7 ch, flat join to 13th dc; 7 ch, flat join to 9th dc; 7 ch, flat join to 5th ch; 7 ch, flat join to 1st ch;
R to L: *4 dc over last 7 ch, P, 4 dc over same 7 ch. Repeat from * for 3 other sets of 7 ch. 4 dc over the next 3 ch sp.
This completes 1 crown. Repeat from * along the whole outline.

Daisy Edging: (Multiple of two 5 ch spaces on a {1 dc, 5 ch, miss 5 sts} band.)
P = 5 chain picot.
*R to L: (4 dc, P, 4 dc)2;
L to R: 9 ch, flat join to st between 5 ch sps; 9 ch, flat join to st before 1st 5 ch sp;
R to L: 5 dc, P, 7 dc over the 2nd 9 ch, 6 dc over 1st 9 ch;
L to R: 11 ch, flat join to dc before picot over 2nd 9 ch;
R to L: 5 dc, P, 5 dc, P, 5 dc over 11 ch, 1 dc, P, 5 dc over the rest of the 1st 9 ch.
Repeat from * along the whole outline.

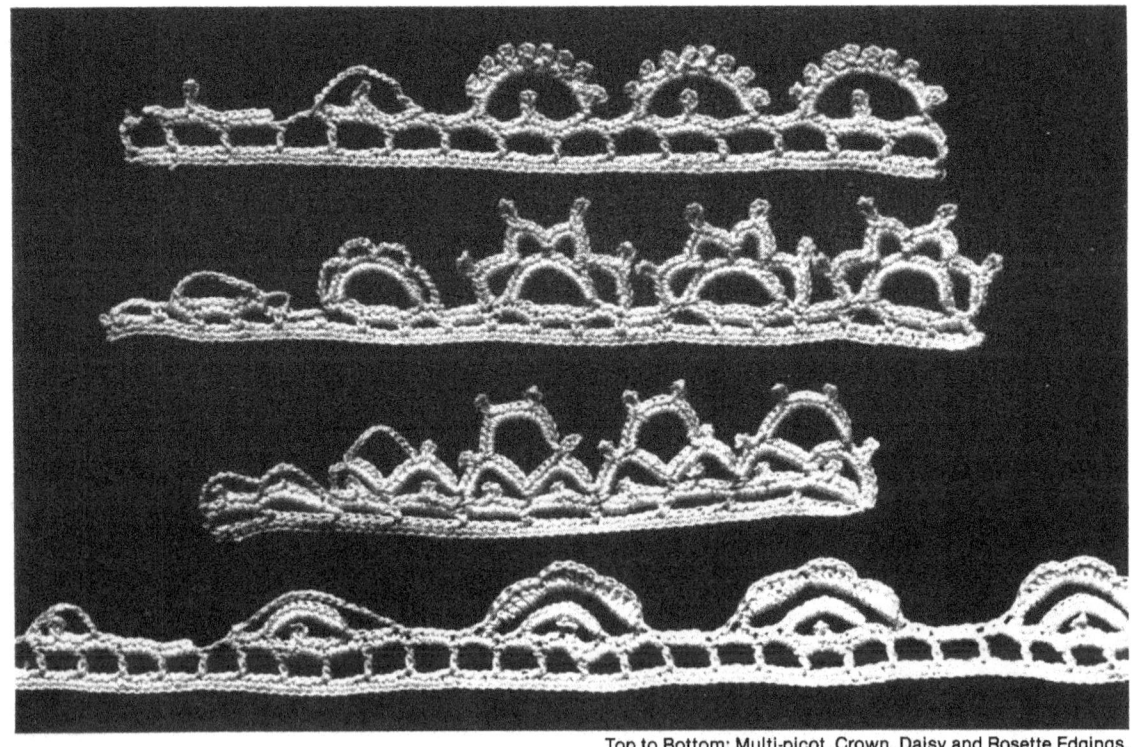

Top to Bottom: Multi-picot, Crown, Daisy and Rosette Edgings.

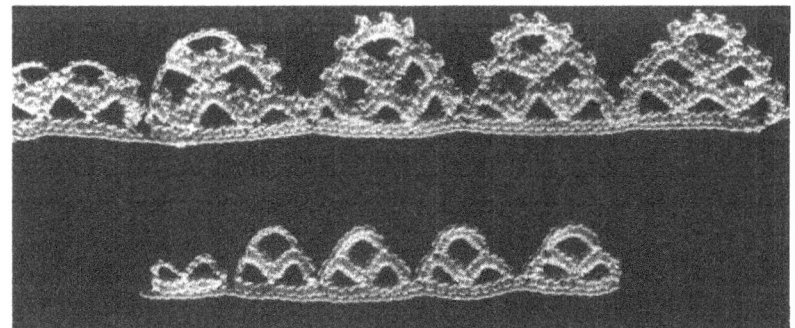

Six-Loop Edging above, Three-Loop Edging below.

Rosette Edging: (Multiple of six 3 ch spaces worked on a {1 tr, 3 ch, miss 3 sts} band.)
P = 5 ch picot.
*R to L: (4 dc over 3 ch sp)3, (2 dc, 1 P, 2 dc) over next 3 ch sp, 2 dc;
L to R: 8 ch, flat join to centre of 3 ch sp to left of P;
R to L: cover 8 ch with dc, 2 dc over remainder of 3 ch sp, 2 dc over next 3 ch sp;
L to R: 18 ch, flat join to centre of second group of 3 ch sp beyond P;
R to L: (1 dc, 5 tr)3 over 18 ch sp, 1 dc; 2 dc over remaining part of 3 ch sp.
Repeat from * the beginning along the whole outline.

Three-Loop Edging: (Worked over Foundation Chain Outline.)
Start with yarn at any part of the outline chain.
*R to L: 8 dc over chain;
L to R: 6 ch, flat join to 5th dc just worked; 6 ch, flat join to 1st dc worked;
R to L: 7 dc over 1st ch sp, 4 dc over 2nd ch sp;
L to R: 6 ch, flat join to centre of 1st ch sp, working 1 dc into 4th dc;
R to L: 7 dc over ch sp just made, 3 dc over 1st ch sp, 1 dc over foundation ch.
Repeat from the beginning until the chain is covered.

Six-Loop Edging with Picots: (Worked over a Foundation Chain Outline.)
P = 3 ch picot (make 3 ch, ss to first ch to make a picot).
*R to L: 13 dc;
L to R: (7 ch)3, flat joining each ch sp to 9th, 5th and 1st dc made;
R to L: {1 dc, (P, 2 dc)3, P, 1 dc}2 over first two 7 ch sps, (1 dc, P, 2 dc, P, 1 dc) over 3rd ch sp;
L to R: (7 ch)2, flat joining each ch sp to centre of 1st and 2nd 6 ch sps (between the picots);
R to L: {1 dc, (P, 2 dc)3, P, 1 dc}, (1 dc, P, 2 dc, P, 1 dc) over the two 7 ch sps;
R to L: 7 ch, flat join to centre of 5th ch sp made (between the picots);
L to R: {1 dc, (P, 2 dc)3, P, 1 dc} in ch sp just made, (1 dc, P, 1 dc) in remaining space of each of next 2 ch sps, 1 dc.
Repeat from the beginning until the chain is covered.

BBREVIATIONS

NOTE: Capital letters for crochet stitches denote working through top (back) loop only.

If a number follows a set of instructions in brackets, that set of instructions is repeated that number of times.

* means repeat the instruction after an asterisk (*), or between asterisks, as directed or until the last few stitches or the end of the row or round.

ch	= chain, chains		dc(DC)	= double crochet
dcb	= double crochet into back		dcc	= double crochet chain
dcj	= double crochet join		DPB	= double picot chain bar
dtr (DTR)	= double treble		htr(HTR)	= half treble
LC	= leave cord		LHS	= left hand side
L to R	= work from left to right		P	= chain picot
lp	= loop		Pb	= ch picot worked L to R
RHS	= right hand side		R to L	= work from right to left
SPB	= single picot chain bar		TC	= tighten cord
tr (TR)	= treble		tr tr (TR TR)	= triple treble
st (sts)	= stitch, stitches		sp (sps)	= space, spaces
ss (SS)	= slip stitch		UC	= use cord
UCA	= use cord alone		yrh	= yarn round hook

THE HERITAGE OF KNITTING SERIES

TESSA LORANT
WWW.TESSALORANTWARBURG.COM

TESSA LORANT'S COLLECTION OF KNITTED LACE EDGINGS
PAPERBACK: ISBN 978-0-906374-50-4

KNITTED QUILTS & FLOUNCES
PAPERBACK: ISBN 978-0-906374-29-0

KNITTED LACE COLLARS
PAPERBACK: ISBN 978-0-906374-51-1

KNITTED SHAWLS & WRAPS
PAPERBACK: ISBN 978-0-906374-52-8

THE SECRETS OF IRISH CROCHET LACE
PAPERBACK: ISBN 978-0-906374-53-5

KNITTED LACE DOILIES
PAPERBACK: ISBN 978-0-906374-28-3

THE THORN PRESS
WWW.THETHORNPRESS.COM

BOOKS IN PRINT

FICTION

THE DOHLEN INHERITANCE TRILOGY
Tessa Lorant Warburg
WWW.TESSALORANTWARBURG.COM

THE DOHLEN INHERITANCE
Paperback: ISBN 978-0-906374-06-1
Hardback: ISBN 978-0-906374-03-0

HOBGOBLIN GOLD
Paperback: ISBN978-0-906374-08-5

LADYBIRD FLY
Paperback: ISBN 978-0-906374-09-2

A WOMAN'S WORLD, 138-9 Chri Plus
Hilary Jerome
WWW.THETHORNPRESS.COM
Paperback: ISBN 978-0-906374-00-9
e-book: ISBN 978-0-906374-36-8

THE MASTER'S TALE, A TITANIC GHOST STORY
ANN VICTORIA ROBERTS
WWW.ANNVICTORIAROBERTS.CO.UK
PAPERBACK: ISBN 978-0-906374-21-4
E-BOOK: ISBN 978-0-906374-39-9

THE GIRL FROM THE LAND OF SMILES
TESSA LORANT WARBURG
WWW.TESSALORANTWARBURG.COM
PAPERBACK: ISBN 978-0-906374-30-6
E-BOOK: ISBN 978-0-906374-41-2

SPELLBINDER
TESSA LORANT WARBURG
WWW.TESSALORANTWARBURG.COM
PAPERBACK: ISBN 978-0-906374-31-3
E-BOOK: ISBN 978-0-906374-35-1

THOU SHALT NOT KILL
TESSA LORANT WARBURG
WWW.TESSALORANTWARBURG.COM
PAPERBACK: ISBN 978-0-906374-28-3
E-BOOK: ISBN 978-0-906374-29-0

CLONER
Emma Lorant
www.thethornpress.com
Paperback: ISBN 978-0-906374-32-0
e-book: ISBN 978-0-906374-33-7

NON FICTION

SNACK YOURSELF SLIM
Richard Warburg & Tessa Lorant
http://www.buypatential.com
Paperback: ISBN 978-0-906374-05-4
e-book: ISBN 978-0-906374-37-5

LOCAL WRITERS

WORDFALL
The 2010 Anthology from Southampton Writing Buddies
Editor Penny Legg
http://www.pennylegg.com
Paperback: ISBN 978-0-906374-26-9

THORN CONTEMPORARY ARTISTS

BRUSHSTROKES TO SPONGES
Richard Warburg
www.buypatential.com
Hardback: ISBN 978-0-906374-43-6
Paperback: ISBN 978-0-906374-40-5

e-book: ISBN 978-0-906374-42-9SOMERSET SCENES
Teil
www.thethornpress.com
Hardback: ISBN 978-0-906374-45-0
Paperback: ISBN 978-0-906374-28-3
e-book: ISBN 978-0-906374-34-4

INKTASTIC
Andrew P Jones
www.thethornpress.com
Paperback: ISBN 978-0-906374-04-7

www.ingramcontent.com/pod-product-compliance
Lightning Source LLC
Chambersburg PA
CBHW081459040426
42446CB00016B/3318